Social Media Branding for Small Business: The 5-Sources Model

Social Media Branding for Small Business: The 5–Sources Model

A Manifesto for Your Branding Revolution

Robert Davis, PhD

BUSINESS EXPERT PRESS

Social Media Branding for Small Business: The 5–Sources Model
Copyright © Business Expert Press, LLC, 2015.

All rights reserved. No part of this publication may be reproduced, stored in a retrieval system, or transmitted in any form or by any means—electronic, mechanical, photocopy, recording, or any other except for brief quotations, not to exceed 400 words, without the prior permission of the publisher.

First published in 2015 by
Business Expert Press, LLC
222 East 46th Street, New York, NY 10017
www.businessexpertpress.com

ISBN-13: 978-1-63157-098-8 (paperback)
ISBN-13: 978-1-63157-099-5 (e-book)

Business Expert Press Digital and Social Media Marketing and Advertising Collection

Collection ISSN: 2333-8822 (print)
Collection ISSN: 2333-8830 (electronic)

Cover and interior design by S4Carlisle Publishing Services Private Ltd., Chennai, India

First edition: 2015

10 9 8 7 6 5 4 3 2 1

Printed in the United States of America.

Dedication

Save the community!
"Some businesses are not sure what to discuss on their social networking pages. They just bombard us with specials and try to sell their products and services. To me social media is not about selling. It's about the link. Building and engaging likeminded people with your brand."
drrobertdavis.com

Table of Contents

Acknowledgment..........*xi*
Preface..........*xiii*
    Power And Validity xiv
    Key Questions xv
Chapter 1   Why, What, and How? 1
    Community Reboot 1
    First Source: Function—Shared Meaning and Objective 2
    Second Source: Emotion and Your brand Loves Me 3
    Third Source: Self-Oriented Actualization 5
    Fourth Source: Personal and Social Engagement 7
    Fifth Source: Collective Relationships 8
    Next Steps 10
Chapter 2   The Importance of Social Media Branding 11
    Brand as App 11
    What is a Social Media Community? 13
    The Social Media Brand and Your Brand 15
    Functional vs. Emotional 19
    Relationships and Community 21
    Closing Thoughts on the Importance of Social Media Branding 23
Chapter 3   Source 1: Functional Social Media Brand 25
    Problem Solving, Information Search, and Feedback 25
    Prompt Action 31
    Convenience and Accessibility 32
    Knowledge 33
    Rewards 34
    Closing Thoughts on the Functional Brand 35
Chapter 4   Source 2: Emotional Social Media Brand 39
    Enjoyment 39
    Problem Alleviation 41

		Privilege 42
		Fantasy 43
		Curiosity 43
		Closing Thoughts on the Emotional Brand 44
Chapter 5		Source 3: Self-Oriented Social Media Brand 49
		Self-Actualization 49
		Self-Relevance 50
		Self-Branding 51
		Life Arrangements 53
		Closing Thoughts on the Self-Oriented Brand 54
Chapter 6		Source 4: Personal (Social) Media Brand 59
		Experience Exchange 59
		Community Attachment 61
		Link Building 62
		Social Engagement 64
		Closing Thoughts on the Personal Brand 64
Chapter 7		Source 5: Relational Social Media Brand 69
		Personalized Brand Communication 69
		Fickle Relational Bonds 71
		Obliged Relational Bonds 72
		Preexisting Relational Bonds 73
		Emerged Relational Bonds 74
		Casual Relational Bonds 75
		Closing Thoughts on the Relational Brand 75
Chapter 8		Implementing Social Media Branding 81
		Create Functionality Through Product
		I Love, Service I Use 81
		Create Emotion By Tapping Into My Feelings 82
		Create The Personal and Social 84
		Create Relationship 85
		Being Interactive and Personal 86
		Closing Thoughts 87
Chapter 9		Brand Building in Action 91
		Case 1 Yarns With Erica and Jess 92
		Case 2 Westjet Xmas Cheer 94
		Case 3 Fun with Bitstrips 95

Case 4 Communication and Social Media......................97
Case 5 Banking and Social Media 98
Case 6 Offline Engagement and Online Community........99
Case 7 The Human Factor...100
Case 8 Not Much Spark in Spark.co.nz 101

Suggestion Readings *105*
Index *117*

Acknowledgment

I would like to acknowledge the contribution of Inna Piven to this book and her significant coauthoring of the first edition. Thanks also to reviewers including Jason Kemp who provided sound practical advice. It was also great to gain the contribution of Michael Breazeale and the words of encouragement from Francesca Dall'Olmo Riley an early pioneer in branding.

Thanks also to the Business Expert Press and Victoria L. Crittenden, Professor & Chair, Marketing Division, Babson College for their vision for social media branding and small business.

I also acknowledge the many scholars who have done research on many areas covered in this book. They are impossible to name them all. Most of this work is outside of the discipline of social media branding, but I have tried to direct the reader to key seminal papers. Starting their journey of understanding! A suggested reading list is also provided at the end of the book. But, this just scratches the surface of the amount of great work that is available. My suggestion to you the reader is: dig deeper.

Thank you to my family and friends who always supported me throughout this process. Mum, Dad, Stella, Dede, Janine as well as Cindy and Icis.

Preface

Social media branding provides the thinking, evidence, and practice to create a road map for practitioners in small businesses to develop and implement their brand in online and offline communities. It provides a start point because one of the biggest issues for small businesses is where to start. I have talked to so many business practitioners who don't like the idea of social media. Often, they say: "We can't do that because of the legal implications! Or, "We will have to employ more people and we don't have the resources."

What they are really saying is: Where do we start? This book provides a framework to start. It is not resource intensive or nowhere is it a legal framework. But it is a framework to guide your strategy and implementation. So, let's start!

The approach is called the *5-Sources Model*. The *five Sources* are the five fundamental branding principles that focus on simply outsourcing your brand. Putting the customer back in control while focusing on the community and this group of dedicated customers and other stakeholders. The *5-Sources Model* is not rocket science or even difficult. It simply says that the social media brand for small businesses needs to play an important role in your customers' functional and emotional existence. It is both the serious and the fun experience of your brand.

But have you asked whether your brand is relevant to the customer at an individual level within the community context? Like a mirror it should reflect the customers' desires and future that often reflect their collective. Finally, your brand helps to define a customer's personal and relationship based engagement[1]. That is just a fancy way of saying your friends and contacts. The community! In other words, it is the stuff that happens in the community both on and offline.

---

[1] *See* for example, Brodie, R. J., Hollebeek, L. D., Juric, B., and Ilic, A. (2011a). "Customer Engagement: Conceptual Domain, Fundamental Propositions, and Implications for Research," *Journal of Service Research* 14, no. 3 (2011a): 252–71.

Power and Validity

The power and validity of the *5-Sources Model* is in the way it was developed. The approach is based on three strong pillars of work on online branding over the last 20 years. You could say that the *5-Sources Model* is the culmination of all that work.

First, let's go back to the inception in 1997, when I started the journey to explore, conceptualize, and measure product and service branding online[2]. The work also includes studies on branding when channels of customer engagement are coupled together. Much of this work has been published and debated in peer-reviewed journals and conferences. This 20 year journey of experience has also included many others. A whole lot of evidence based work and research on branding has been with my colleagues such as Inna Piven, Bodo Lang, Rod Brodie, Margo Buchanan-Oliver, and Peter Danaher.

Second, to evolve and further confirm that work, feedback was recently gained from customers in social media about their engagement with brands in everyday life. Here I teamed up with Inna Piven to do this work. In this book I share a lot of that feedback and help practically explain the *5-Sources Model* and its subcomponents. I think we are pretty honored to have access to this customer-based resource. I always believe in practice and theory that the best business models are based on sound customer feedback and experience. The *5-Sources Model* is evidence based, that is, it is an approach based upon what customer think and do.

Finally, the *5-Sources Model* provides practical orientation and insight. I am tired of reading the work of others based upon opinion, which is like hollow log, without substance. This book is based on what the social media community wants, what they told me, without bias, prejudice, or agenda. It is their call for ownership of your brand. This work is also based on the small business: the business owner is the team. Yes, I am going to cite some large company examples. But don't get too tied up on that.

---

[2] This early work provided direction and inspration: De Chernatony, L., and Dall'Olmo Riley, F. D. "Experts' Views About Defining Brands and the Principles of Services Branding." *Journal of Business Research* 46, no. 2 (1999): 181–92. http://www.sciencedirect.com.

The principles are largely the same. The *5-Sources Model* also suggests to the business owner that they start to build their team. But, not in the traditional way. Rather, outsourcing social media brand functions and role to their customers and other stakeholders.

The *5-Sources Model* together with this journey and current work on your brand in social media, contributes to the thinking and practice. A lot of companies are using social media, but many of them fail to build relationships and position their brands as community assets. Now, build the concept of your brand in social media by focusing on the development of five important sources of value for customers. In essence it signals the day when your brand is owned by the community. It is outsourced to the customer and other stakeholders in the social media community.

Key Questions

In summary, the *5-Sources Model* approach asks the following questions of your brand and its stakeholders:

- *Functional:* What is the role of your brand in enabling customer objectives and how can we put them back in control? Further, how can the community be enveloped into this process of value creation?
- *Emotional:* How does your brand facilitate the customers' acknowledgment of their feelings and their daily dose of emotional value? Can friends and family become involved in your brand emotive impact and consequences?
- *Self:* Is your brand important to the customer own image of their self? How can your brand engage them with other community members to help guide them through their journey as a customer?
- *Personal:* How does your brand foster and nurture a customer's social linkages? Friends and family play an important role, but how can a brand leverage social relationships to become that Lovemark[3]?

---

[3] *See* http://www.lovemarks.com/.

- *Relational:* What is the role of your brand in the community of relationships? Given this role, what type of value does it create and what others stakeholders are part of that relationship equity?

I hope that you enjoy this book and that it contributes value to your brand and community relationships both on and offline.

Kia kaha! (Be strong, get stuck in, and keep going)[4].

---

[4] Maori Dictionary Translation at http://www.maoridictionary.co.nz/word/11337.

CHAPTER 1

Why, What, and How?

Community Reboot

The *5-Sources Model* starts with the fundamental question: Where is your brand? Where does it exist? Before I would have said that it exists within your company, with its people and possibly on the shelf or online. It is articulated in a strategy document. We often see your brand in traditional marketing communications. It is part of the vision.

The *5-Sources Model* says those days are over. What I like to say is that traditional branding has been rebooted by the community. The days when companies had control over the brand are over because something called "the community" has broken free from its offline cage. Like antimatter, the community and its offline and social media presence have reabsorbed these traditional frameworks and architectures. Like a B grade movie, the community has morphed into an uncontrollable beast. It found online and pushed *go* or maybe *on* is a better word.

The community just rebooted business and their primary target has been . . . yes, you guessed it, the brand. Offline, their views were mostly ignored or hidden in market research studies on the brand. Now their input into the brand and its meaning is ubiquitous and in real-time nano-second mode. Multilingual, multidevice, and multichannel. All interlinked with extreme velocity and synchronicity.

What is the 5-Sources Model?

The community ownership of the brand expressed through the function, emotional, actualization, personal, social and relational.

The first change on the agenda is the meaning of the brand. Now it is purely from the customers' perspective. Brand meaning is now owned by the community and we aren't going back. That community involves many different brand stakeholders and could involve customers, businesses, suppliers, influencers, social interest groups etc[1].

Given the significant change in how we view and think about your brand, the reboot has motivated the creation of a new way of thinking about the brand. The *5-Sources Model*. Motivated by the movement of the social community. Let's go!

First Source: Function—Shared Meaning and Objective

First, the community has reclaimed your brand and its functional role. This is the first source of the *5-Sources Model*. Brands were originally designed to be a "short-hand" for their customers: The symbolic device of value. Many have lost their way and are driving internal organizational agendas rather than customer value and experience. Hence, the community now owns your brand in the direction, process and outcomes from a functional perspective.

Any good book on branding should cite Google. What a story! Google is a brand worth nearly $300 billion. It is mammoth and nearly as large as a small country. But, what is strange about the brand is that the brand equity has been built up through almost zero expenditure on the traditional black hole of marketing communications. This is pretty confusing because it directly challenges other valuable brands such as Apple and Walmart.

The key is that the brand is built upon the fundamental basis of Google's business model. But what is that foundation? Rather obvious, the stakeholder-users. You! Even the search engine result is a function of your measured behavior. Who you are? Where you live? What are your preferences? Some call this big brother or "big data." The *5-Sources Model*

---

[1] For example, *see* the early work for further reading on brand communities: Cova, B., and Pace, S., "Brand Community of Convenience Products: New Forms of Customer Empowerment—The Case My Nutella The Community," *European Journal of Marketing* 40, no. 9/10 (2006): 1087–105.

sees it as the way the community takes back your brand and controls the functional outcomes. In the case of Google; the brand is functionally driven by the community. What it does, *is the community*.

> ### 5-Sources Model: Function
>
> Moving to high community brand value and collective brand sourcing: Take the brand away from the internal agenda through a revolutionary DE: VORCE. Stolen toward shared ownership by its collective. A new form of shareholder and value.

To help enable the functional aspect of the brand in the *5-Sources Model* your brand might help to facilitate the following shared activities across the community:

- **Material Rewards:** Brand as a priority club enables customers to get exclusive access to the material and tangible rewards.
- **Problem Solving:** Brand as an emergency room focuses on stress free, time and money saving solutions, and enables customers to address problems.
- **Information Search:** Brand as an information center enables customers to find the required information about your brand, alternatives or expert advice.
- **Knowledge:** Brand as a search engine and a data center enables customers to manage knowledge about your brand in a convenient way.
- **Feedback:** Brand as a conference room enables customers to express their opinions directly to your brand.

Second Source: Emotion and Your brand Loves Me

Emotion! This is the second source of the *5-Sources Model*. Emotion is centered on the community's acknowledgment of its community and social self[2]. That it exists off and online. One of the major issues your brand faces here is the lack of congruency or fit between your brand and its image in social media vs. the community image of its stakeholders. This occurs because brands outside the community structure are often run under traditional managerial and control approaches.

When they become involved in social media branding they apply the same model. Sure you can have rules. Digital has always been about netiquette. But brands that operate by control and command in relational community structures just seem disjointed and out of the play and flow of the community and where it wants to take your brand. The lack of fit destroys the emotional connection. Think about whether emotion is a planned outcome of a community's engagement with a brand? No! It can't be. Emotion can't be planned.

> ### 5-Sources Model: Emotion
>
> Moving to high community brand value and collective brand sourcing: Transforming brand emotion from destruction of the fit with the planned direction toward love defined by connection.

Let's look at the case of Apple. What I get about Apple is not just their design or great leadership. I think we can find many examples of this across the globe, small and large. What Steve Jobs did understand, apart from his employees and stakeholders in their brand, was brand emotion. So much so because the community simply loves the Apple brand. I think that was the secret. It is not really about the design or Steve himself. You are just an Apple person or not. If you are an Apple person then you are not alone. You are part of a community or what I like to call a subculture. Hence, it is that community and the activities between members that

---

[2] For example, *see* the early work of Hirschman, E. C., and Holbrook, M. B.," Hedonic consumption: Emerging concepts, methods and propositions," *Journal of Marketing* 46, (1982): 92–101.

underlie brand emotion. What is true is that emotion will have many different forms and outcomes. Often it will be hedonically for the sake of its existence. Some examples of the role of emotion in the *5-Sources Model* could be:

- **Curiosity:** Brand as an object of curiosity. By holding a curiosity value brand makes customers want to uncover your brand.
- **Enjoyment:** Brand as a source of enjoyable and exciting experiences that make customers feel happy and satisfied.
- **Fantasy:** Brand as a form of customer escapism, desired reality and aspirations offering exciting and unusual experiences.
- Entertainment: Brand as a source of entertainment. By giving customers amusement and interest brand makes them enjoy their experiences.
- Privilege/ Recognition: Brand as the source of reassurance that customers are noticed and appreciated by a brand.
- Problem Alleviation: Brand as a source of help given to customers to deal with difficult personal situations.

Third Source: Self-Oriented Actualization

The third source of the *5-Sources Model* is the self. Here we move beyond acknowledgment to actualization. We move from your brand in social media defining our shared relationship and emotion (your brand mirrors me and the community)—toward pushing through to, *your brand is me*. No separation between what your brand is, or should be. It is just me![3].

The state of actualization is at the highest point of value for the community. As you will read later, your brand and its related strategies, tactics, and conversations permeate the individual customer's own personal relationships on and offline. They become a permanent part of the fabric of what defines a customer from a social media perspective.

---

[3] *See* for example Houston, M. B., and Walker, B. A., "Self-Relevance and Purchase Goals: Mapping a Consumer Decision," *Journal of the Academy of Marketing Science* 24, no. 3 (1996): 232–45.

> ### 5-Sources Model: Actualisation (SELF)
>
> Moving to high community brand value and collective brand sourcing: Not more about you (the brand) and US (together). Rather, ME. I am the brand and my collective, together we are the SELF. U + US does not exist without ME.

Facebook has taken actualization to the extreme, as customers can now be defined by their choices across brands in music, movies, and other content. Another example is me, my gardening, and Zoodoo[4]. Zoodoo is essentially compost made from the poo or Zoo animals. Giraffe, zebra, elephant, bison, antelope, llama, rhino, hippo, and camel. I buy it for my vegetable garden and I just bought 10 40-liter bags for this summer's garden. It arrived today and you know the first things I thought about was sharing this event on Facebook. Crazy! But why? Self actualization and the Zoodoo brand. Taking my experience offline, online into the social media. I want my friends to know through the Zoodoo brand that I am a good, but cool gardener. In essence, not a lot of separation between the brand and me. When you come to my house for dinner, you will know that the vegetables are grown from something very special, not to mention supporting environmental sustainability.

> ### 5-Sources Model: Personal/Social
>
> Moving to high community brand value and collective brand sourcing: The collective takes the brand back to the native social interaction. From the offline freedom through psychic prison of legacy architecture.

---

[4] *See* http://www.zoodoo.co.nz/.

When these brands are absorbed into an individual's self-actualization they may take different forms and play disparate roles. For example, they may be involved in:

- **Life Arrangements:** Brand as a source of support for customers to simplify or facilitate their day-to-day activities.
- **Self-Relevance:** Brand as a link to the customers' sense of self. Customers get involved with a brand that fits well with their personal/professional interests and life style.
- **Self-Branding:** Brand as a platform for the customers' self-branding and building and raising their social profiles.
- **Self-Actualization:** Brand as a source of support for customers to achieve what they want through their relationships with brands.
- **Expression:** Brand as a vehicle for self-expression, allowing the customers to publicly present their thoughts and ideas and let others know who and what they are.

Fourth Source: Personal and Social Engagement

Before a brand within the *5-Sources Model* can evolve toward a community relationship I need to acknowledge the reality of the customer's need for social engagement. This is the fourth source of the *5-Sources Model*. Everyone understands that people need social engagement. Offline, social engagement is all around us. It is what we do and how we work. However, the Internet kind of destroyed social engagement for a number of reasons, but mostly because it is machine generated and controlled like a physical prison. For years key demographics such as female customers have avoided buying and interacting online. Why? Because the social experience conflicts with what is natural and normal.

5-Sources Model: Relationship

Moving to high community brand value and collective brand sourcing: Traditional relationships are so defined by controlled trust, commitment and respective. The collective moves toward brand value defined by the random gate-crash. BANG!

Then along came social media services like LinkedIn, which allow professionals to connect in an instinctive or native way. I also had to laugh at the very symbolic movie, *Her*. Taking personal engagement, socialness, and technology to the next level of intuition. A movie about the man who falls in love with his OS. But don't laugh so hard. Technology, being led by the social media and its community-based learning will evolve to that point where we will interact with it on a natural and interactive level. The entity will be synchronous and contingent in the way that it interacts. Your brand will also evolve.

In its way, LinkedIn enhances this social process. Your brand helps to facilitate the different types of exchange, such as:

- **Experience Exchange:** Brand as a service for the exchange of experiences, ideas, and know-how between customers.
- **Sociality:** Brand as a meeting platform that gives customers a place to talk.
- **Link Building:** Brand as a source of customer networking for personal or professional interests.
- **Community Attachment:** Brand as a community hub where customer experiences are formed, shared, and communicated.

Fifth Source: Collective Relationships

Finally, the Fifth S. The *5-Sources Model* also defines the community relationship of a community. When you situate your brand in a Facebook page, linking it to other social media technologies, as well as the invited and uninvited random gatecrashers, the brand relationships start to revolve around those community objectives and experiences[5]. That is a hard one to get. The best analogy is that your brand is now partly defined by a complex and noisy space. A big part of that meaning will be content-based.

For example, as Hershey's Milk Chocolate, with over 6 million likes on Facebook states: "Welcome to the Hershey's Page on Facebook!

---

[5] *See* the work of Fournier, S., "Consumers and their Brands: Developing Relationship Theory in Consumer Research," *Journal of Consumer Research* 24, (1998): 343–73.

We encourage you to interact with us by leaving comments, photos, and videos[6]." In essence, their brand and its meaning and value to the community are content-based. The type of relationship between the brand and community is a type of content-based brand conversation.

The *5-Sources Model* proposes that there will be many different types of relationships within the community. For example, some may be:

- **Emerged:** The form of relationships occurring for the first time in social media and based on online experiences only.
- **Casual:** The form of relationships resulting from accidental or irregular experiences regardless of the online or offline context.
- **Preexisting:** The form of relationships resulting from the customers' prior brand knowledge and experiences.
- Obliged: The form of relationships resulting from statutory obligations, not because they are wanted or desirable.
- **Fickle:** The form of relationships that is temporary and often bonded by the present situation.

The key objective for your brand is to determine two things. First, what types of relationships exist with my brand in social media? How do they create or erode community value?

Understanding 5-Sources Model?

To move from flat world transactional branding toward the 5S Model there are six key steps. <u>1 and 2:</u> Understand why the social media brand is important and what it is? <u>3 and 4:</u> Define and implement the 5S Model. Finally, <u>5 and 6:</u> Optimize interactivity across channels and collective connections.

---

[6] *See* https://www.facebook.com/HERSHEYS.

Next Steps

The next steps in the book, having briefly summarized the *5-Sources Model* are three-fold. First, I am going to talk about the importance of branding and social media. This will be an exploration of some of the hot topic both now and in the past. Second, we get to the heart of the *5-Sources Model* and the following five chapters work through each source component of the model and its subcomponents. Customer feedback and conversations that were had about real social media branding will be shared so that you can understand how to reinterpret your branding strategy in social media community.

Finally, we end the book through a discussion about implementation and application. This will be accompanied by a "think" chapter which will provide seven fresh case studies with questions you can work through. I would encourage you to go to drrobertdavis.com to provide feedback on the questions. Here I can then help.

CHAPTER 2

The Importance of Social Media Branding

In this chapter we are going to explore the importance of social media branding. This is going to cover a range of different topics that just tend to highlight issues and trends. We will start with the new definition of a brand as app in social media. This will then help us to the next stage of understanding: what is a social media community and how is it transforming branding into the social media brand? As part of that transformation I am then going to conclude the discussion by focusing on two important issues; functional vs. emotional branding and the brand as a collective.

Brand as App

In 1980, Alvin Toffler forecast that electronic cottages would dramatically change society, challenging the way people think, work, and live. Now as predicted, the cottage has broken free in the world of space that we, our brands and other stakeholders' community occupy. Disney is no longer restricted to its theme parks, retail stores, or even online space. Disney's community can now exist where its stakeholders are.

> ### Brand as application
>
> Simultaneous coupling of channels of interactivity and experience. Offline, Online U-Space . . . (where ever). Sharing content creation and process. Roles are diffuse. Stakeholders. Collective and community oriented. Uncontrolled and controlled (guarded).

Like Disney your brand can become ubiquitous. This new space is loosely called Social Media. For its customers it is truly defined by its ability to create unlimited opportunities for engagement—beyond the cottage: anytime and from anywhere. It is where stakeholders of your brand can engage in a personalized and continuous way.

There have been many reports that argue for social media transformation. Many argue that social media provides a world of connections. Pointing out that social media communities have become not only common public spaces, but also channels of influence that is often translated into transactions. eMarketer reports that the population of social networks users will exceed 2.55 billion by the end of 2017[1]. eMarketer strongly argues that many of these users are using social media because of the rapid growth in different Internet and mobile applications, which has strengthened the connection between brand and customer[2]. Hence, more social media users are engaging with their social community and making purchase decision. So, you ask: Why is our brand not engaging in these opportunities?

> "Now it is less what the advertiser says and what the brand is. Now it is more what the brand means to customers, with that meaning increasingly derived through social media"

There is no doubt that this wave of change is being fueled by the needs of businesses and customers looking for more opportunities of engagement through brand-related conversations in social media. Buying has moved on from the transaction. Now the customers of Walmart want to talk directly to your brand. They want engagement through conversation. Importantly, this conversation involves other stakeholders from your brand's

---

[1] Emarketer, [http://www.emarketer.com/Article/Social-Networking-Reaches-Nearly-One-Four-Around-World/1009976]

[2] *See* for example the work of Balasubramanian, S., Peterson R. A., and Javenpaa S. L., "Exploring the Implications of M-Commerce For Markets and Marketing," *Journal of Academy of Marketing Science* 30, no.4 (2002): 348–61.

community—this is why Facebook has exploded. Brand related communication has become interactive conversation that is relevant and engaging.

This is exciting and I could go on about who is using it and why. But we sort of know that already. So, let's get to the heart of the issue here, that is, the customers' migration into social media has already had far-reaching consequences for brands but there has been little thinking about the social media brand. This is a significant issue because now the customer does not care about traditional advertising. In fact they have switched off and turned onto what other customers are saying on social media about brand.

This can be a pretty scary proposition for the likes of Target and Woolworths in the retail sector. Their traditional brand model is firmly based on shouting at customers every night on television. The key message: here is the price now. Buy *now*! What I am arguing here that communication is now engagement which is a conversation amongst your brand stakeholders, regardless of whether Target and Woolworths want it that way. *Wow.* The time has truly arrived. Stakeholders are in the driving seat of brand value. So, rather than ignoring this revolution, let's start to understand what it is. The first step is to briefly discuss what a social media community is.

What is a Social Media Community?

There are lots of ways of viewing a social media community but let's start with a purely functional perspective. Well really it is just an Internet-based application based on three simple principles. First, it can be deployed across many devices. So long as it can connect to the Internet then I am in business. Second, it must seamlessly connect people. Not randomly, but with people that are part of their community. Finally, it must be able to facilitate the creation and exchange of many types of customer generated content. Yes, even that photo of your cat smiling!

Social Media Community?

$SMC = C \pm C \pm E$
CCE is Content, Community, Exchange

The important principles here are threefold; content, community, and exchange, or CCE. Technology isn't the key issue here. A social media community exists because the community wants to exchange content. So, lucky for Fox we want to share our Simpsons pictures with our community. But the reality is that social media community is one of those stupid realizations that CCE is what people just do anyway.

However, your brands have gotten confused because social media communities are just treated like additional sales or advertising channels. You just have to look at the debate that surrounded Facebook when it listed in 2012. Most of the discussion about the business was focused on advertising revenue. Such a view is the polar opposite of CCE. In fact it is cold. Some have bucked the trend and understand that CCE means that stakeholders want to acquire knowledge and branding experiences within social media. But most of all they want to take control of your brands source of value themselves. Social media communities have transformed consumers from the passive to the noisy riotous community into linking places where brands that are valued support social engagement and community.

I also like the view that social media community is excessive. Even though the CCE has a functional role it exists sometimes purely for an excess of hedonic experience. Why just play Scrabble with one player online? Play with 25 at the same time. Ubiquitous action through my Samsung or Apple device.

I also like the theme of equality and democracy, not in a traditional way but defined by CCE. It brings into force the needs of stakeholders who are more like pivotals in their roles are diffuse. Now that is an interesting word, pivotal. What does it mean? Well, a pivotal is a bit like a thought leader but they do more than that. They are special participants in social media community. You will know and see them in your own community. They are the individuals who seem to be able to facilitate the conversation toward action. Often they specialize in a particular topic (e.g., organizing football on Saturday). They in essence live and breathe with their community; content, community, and exchange. What makes them very powerful is their ability to engage in CCE across different vertical channels of engagement (e.g., mobile, web, radio, tv, etc) and horizontally across communities (e.g., they are often active and a key part of many communities).

I think the key to their success for your brand is that they are really good at creating engagement through content across channels and exchange between community members. Pivotals are also seamless in social media markets because they democratize knowledge and information. As part of this equality between brand and customer, pivotals and the community don't consume, they create. Content and exchange is their heat and their contribution to the value of your brand. This momentum is being driven by the desire of increasing participation of consumers in what your brand is and what it means. So, why not let them? Pivotals are the hot spots for your brand I promise.

With CCE there is also the important theme of real time exchange, which is often taken for granted. There is a move toward the real time brand experience as defined by CCE. In this respect, it is logical to suggest that for customers, being a member of a social media community and engaging with brands using web-based and mobile media, is very compelling. Think about traditional product brands like Pepsi and IKEA. Before social media the experience was oriented around a flat world related to usage. You had to use the brand to experience it. Now through CCE your brand stakeholders in a social media community leverage the experiences of others.

They key question though is, given we have CCE, how has this transformed your brand?

The Social Media Brand and Your Brand

Linking to the concept of CCE I argue that the social media brand is continuously evolving and constructed by the community and its stakeholders. For example, the value that arises from CCE related brand engagement is often described as experiences or performances, deeds or processes, and interactions, a relationship fulcrum and a promise. Whatever you want to call it the core theme of these outcomes of value and what actually is the social media brand is that the stakeholders are brand cocreators. This is a real challenge for traditional marketers as your brand in social media involves engagement with a broader group of stakeholders, and this process involves them as coproducers. In other words they are equal to you. They make and contribute to the brand and what the brand is in terms of product and/or service or other. Let's not forget about the not-for-profits.

A really interesting example of this is the transformation of a traditional product brand. For the Colgate brand the evolving definition of what their social media brand is can also be further extended and challenged by the unique elements of the service environment, namely intangibility, inseparability of production and consumption, perishability and heterogeneity. This means that a traditional product brand adds to the social media community a strong service component, whether it is wanted or not. For example, the customers and stakeholder of Colgate, through CCE, will often drive and control intangibility and heterogeneity. The way they will create the brand variability and lack of physicalness will be through the social media based conversation, in other words.

But I need to recognize that in social media the most problematic aspect of brand is its intangible nature. This can be really tough on a brand that has been based on brand equity models as "sinks" of value. For example, it is really easy to value the McDonald's brand because it is very tangible in its assets and sales. In the service environment of a social media community, CCE is an intangible activity which often does not result in a transfer of ownership. So, CCE is really hard to encapsulate into brand value. The CCE real time is in seconds and the only place of its reality is the mind of the consumer. To overcome this transience, CCE and a social media community may place a strong emphasis on offline activity to make brands more tangible to consumers.

I think this is where Facebook has really shined in terms of events and social media brand tangibility. Commonly, events are placed on Facebook that have a physical location and time. Let the pivotals to their work. They then beaver away, corralling their community toward the event, that is, if the brand is perceived to be of value. Hence, the event is reality and all that great content created by the brand and the communities get sucked back up into the social media. Confirming tangibly the intangible experience. Hey presto! Your social media brand is now real, relevant, and most of all owned by the pivotals and their clans.

Also, when thinking about a brand in social media I need to focus on consumption. I tried to think of a better word for consumption as it is a pretty ambiguous word when you start thinking about brands. How do we consume a brand? Here is a clear definition.

Most studies on a customer's consumption behavior focus on what people do, think, and feel when they consume. Consumption is viewed as a type of social action and process through which customers make use of and engages with brands in a variety of ways across groups and situations, depending on the objects and purposes of the consumption. So, yeah, if I look at a brand in an advertisement, I am consuming it. The same if I: use it, feel it, share it, avoid it, and possibly even EAT it. Yummy!

One of the really interesting things about your brand in social media is that your stakeholders consume it in a very subjective way. This subjectivity is often not very objective but it is defined by the context of the consumer and community; they are the lens of the individual. Hence, what your brand means when they consume it will depend on whether it subjectively reinforces the customer and communities self-beliefs, social engagements or it helps to discover something new about the self.

Consumption is all really flash but what I get concerned about in the CCE equation of Content, Community, and Exchange is: momentum. Momentum is about maintaining the length and breadth of the conversations that surround your brand that your customers and stakeholders are engaging in. Length is time. Breadth is the number of community members, pivotals, different horizontal communities, and vertical channels of engagement (e.g., mobile, web, radio, tv, etc) your conversations transcend. I think breadth is probably the simplest way of defining viral[3].

So, let's come back to your social media brand conversations. Don't they often run out of steam or have a lack of length and breadth.

The key question then for your social media branding is how to keep the dialogue alive and interactive. Well this is really what this book is all about and we will discuss this in more detail across the *5-Sources Model* but I think customers and the community use your brand and others as offerings to the exchange process and consumption. That is right; often the community will create a conversation and often brands will be used

---

[3] *See* also the work of Breazeale, M., "Word of mouth: An assessment of electronic word-of-mouth research," *International Journal of Market Research* 51, no. 3 (2009): 297–318.

like fuel to the fire. This is because like heat, consumption is an observed and felt phenomenon. We feel it and experience it. So when a group of friends in a community are worn out from sharing photos and other random user created content, they will often resort to brands. These brands represent the fuel of consumption within the community.

One friend might like Volkswagen or NTT Docomo. This exchange and consumption of brand content in the community may have been motivated by two forces. First, the discomfort of consumption wear-out. In other words, there is nothing more to say at that time. To move to a feeling of comfort a customer will share brands that relate to their personal experiences. In this way wear out is distanced and the state of interactivity maintained. Customers and their community look for new types of social engagement beyond the mundane. They look to conversation pivotals to pass along to their family and friends and in this way, social media communities can be viewed as amplified word-of-mouth (WOM) which have a huge impact of other customers' feelings and decision making.

To help us understand this process of consumption we need to think about it from your brand and customers/communities point of view. First, your brand is asking: How do I leverage consumption? Well, this is a tough one because consumption between community members is complex and the basis of exchange is not always apparent.

For example, because I like Honda cars and I bought one yesterday does not mean my community will share the same view. So, it is really hard to predict the rules of exchange consumption unless you can measure them. I think this is where brands need to back off and let the community decide. Have trust in the fundamentals of your brand and its product, service, and organization. If you are creating value and satisfaction then your brand will find its way into the process of community consumption. Sometimes brand that get too directly involved in the conversation disrupt the internal flow. A flow of dialogue which may be pretty random but in some way it means something to the community. Just accept it!

Second, the customer and community view. Here I take a service-dominant logic view which essentially says: the customer and the communities with your brand cocreate the value of your brand and its offerings. Hence, in some ways the role of the customer and their community is to evaluate the value offered and promised by your brand and then: decide, plan, and implement how cocreation will occur. Heavy stuff, but maybe it is as simple as recognizing that what is valued by the customer and community is consumption which is a communal experience. These communal experiences not only define the "group brain" but also in a multitude of ways link customer and community brand use to the self: to differentiate and express their individuality.

Maybe a simple way of thinking about this is the social media driven conversation about the 2014 Soccer World Cup vs. investment in societal infrastructure. It is many things but also includes offline/online protests in Brazil that are fueled by the disgruntled rising middle class who are dissatisfied by government and societal actions. As Aljazeera notes[4]: "Scattered street demonstrations popped up around Brazil for a third day as protesters continued their community cry against the low-quality public services they receive in exchange for high taxes and high prices." The discussion is in both spaces but it becomes polarized in the social media community. The conversations become amplified in terms of the people's cognitive, affective, and behavioral reactions. This spills out into the offline public space where communities then vent their feelings.

Functional vs. Emotional

It is clear that the most discussion by brands and their customers/community tends to focus on the emotional aspects of consumption, since they believe that in the exchange process, emotional experiences like pleasure, joy, and fantasy create brand differentiation and a bond and trust in your brand. In the consumption of the social media brand this focus is important because the flow of CCE is oriented around the personal community. Hence, it is important to view the emotional element of brand experience: brand engagement as deep, enduring connection to your brand that surpasses physical fulfillment. Like fandom and the All Blacks brand. Engagement is a way of life, history and cultural orientation passed down through the family.

---

[4] *See* http://www.aljazeera.com/sport/football/2013/06/2013619121330645419.html.

Questions are also asked about the appropriate value propositions of your brand that engage the customer and community in cocreation. We propose that these could be content related to:

- Entertainment, educational, aesthetic, and escapist experiences (e.g., Pinterest).
- Opportunities for exclusivity.
- Content from other channels (e.g., TV programming).
- A forum for conversation.

Conversely, it is also important to acknowledge the content related to the functional aspect of brand consumption and service qualities. However, what about the balance between emotional and functional elements in brand consumption. There are three parts to the solution.

First, the balance will be determined by the customers' and the community's consumption behavior. Second, it may be dictated by the role of your brand offline, which could play either a more functional or a more remote role in customer value creation. My argument is that in social media consumption, brands that are more emotive in physical markets need to place emphasis in social media on functional reality (and vice versa).

For example, Siemens is a famous German brand renowned for its functional product quality. In social media it can develop the emotional connections, for example, between doctor and patients regarding Siemens medical scanners. The brand becomes more relevant because of its contribution to the health and well-being of its customers, which is shared with their community.

Third, product vs. service vs. not for profit/cause-related. It is my argument that service and not for profit/cause-related suffer from the issue of intangibility. The customer experiences it but can't see it. Often this experience is very emotional and hedonic. Conversely in social media your brand and related content may place more emphasis on the functional element.

The Mayo Clinic is well known for its contribution to the health of patients. Every day lives are saved and transformed. But how? As a service it is hard to see how and by what method. In the social media consumption of the brand, the Mayo Clinic can bring functional reality to this emotion through, for example, content related to customer stories about their service experience. These stories within their community are tagged to the brand and talk specifically about who was involved and what happened. The story of health can also be tracked, added to, shared, and liked.

So, what is more important; the functional or the emotional? The serious or the fun? Answer: Both. In social media branding, both coexist in a mutually beneficial relationship.

Relationships and Community

Up to this point there has been a lot of discussion about your brand in the social media community. But I would now like to draw attention to the community's view of your brand, looking at it through a community lens. In part this is a summary of a few key points. To do this I will focus on two perspectives: relationships and community.

First, in social media branding the community views your brand as a relationship. This view stems from relationship marketing: relationships help to create additional value above the value created by the product or service. Generally speaking, relationship marketing is the effective communication between brands and customers, which influences customers' attitudes and consumption behaviors and, above all, the quality of their relationships with brands. Relationships are a process over time in response to fluctuations in the contextual environment. For example, as discussed before in relation to social media brand consumption and the fluctuations in content and exchange. In this sense, the quality of the relationships is characterized by the degree to which customers feel attached to a brand in terms of relational and emotional factors and self-connections. Your brand as a relationship is important to the community as it facilitates conversation, often on the basis of personalized service communication.

Second, the importance of the community and the brand. The community will often define your brand as being part of a community this approach has a long history in sociological, cultural, and communication research. There are several approaches to the conceptualization of community as locality, social activity, social structure, and as sentiment. But, although communities may differ in many respects, there are two essential indicators: solidarity and significance, which determine the strength of any community.

The idea of brand and community consumption was first proposed by Daniel Boorstin[5] as a group of people brought together by a set of shared inputs, processes, and outputs. Since then, knowledge about brand communities has been developed from studies on the Macintosh, Harley Davidson, Star Trek, and Jeep communities of consumption[6]. In this view your brand represents a type of bond between community members that is the same phenomenon online as well as offline. Brands in communities are defined as a human association around branded goods or services in a structured set of social relationships. It is like a brand related shared consciousness, ritual, and tradition. To put it differently, for a group of people to become a brand community they need to be united by common consumption interests. They are not just people who are lumped together; they are supposedly devoted customers who share a community hierarchy, social norms, and relationships that are formed through consumption activities.

Further, brand communities revolve around everyday activities that help to form a type of subculture. For example, Harley Davidson[7]. The community is cultural and social. All activities revolve around your brand. This brand community has been built to express shared identity but also develop social links through brand affiliations. This brand community is a human affiliation in which a shared passion or interest toward a particular product or consumption activity unites members. Bonded by specific interrelations, brand admirers are intrinsically connected toward members. Commonly accepted norms and rituals and social ties also characterize face-to-face brand communities. Another idea is that a brand community may help members to satisfy a variety of needs, from finding

---

[5] Friedman, M., Abeele, P. V., and De Vos, K., "Boorstin's Consumption Community Concept: A Tale of Two Countries," *Journal of Consumer Policy* 16, no. 1 (1993): 35–60.
[6] *See* for example: Kozinets, R. V., "Utopian Enterprise: Articulating the Meanings of Star Trek's Culture of Consumption," *Journal of Consumer Research* 28, (2001): 67–88.
[7] *See* for example Schouton, J. W., and McAlexander, J. H., "Subcultures of Consumption: an Ethnography of the New Bikers," *Journal of Consumer Research* 22, (1995): 43–61.

information and emotional support to enhancing self-identities. It is well known that brand communities play a vital role in building customer-brand relationships, but do they play the same role in online settings?

Closing Thoughts on the Importance of Social Media Branding

We have just been through a journey to explain the importance of the social media brand. There are a lot of things to think about, but this is what I think is important for the small business before I move forward discuss the *5-Sources Model*: Five Sources of Social Media Brand.

First, start to think about how your brand has changed in social media: moving toward the concept of brand as an app or application. Its role is to optimize the customers interactive experience and brand engagement across all the channels of brand experience engaged in by the customer and other stakeholders (offline and online)[8]. Move your thinking well beyond product and even service. Your brand has legs and it's active.

Second, the social media brands role is diffuse but unlimited: it is oriented around serving the community and community with content in an uncontrolled and controlled way. Traditional brand speak is about control. I think we need to diverge from this and allow our customers to really take control of your brand. Freedom for the brand and customer! What are we afraid of? A customer's negative comment? Don't they do that anyway?

Third, brand communications in social media is less about traditional advertising and more about being turned on by what other customers are saying. Word of mouth WOM amplified. People just don't watch TV anymore and when they are what are they doing? Probably on their mobiles? When mostly? Probably in the advertisement break. Why? Because traditional advertising is boring. Think about this for a moment.

---

[8] *See* for example, Davis, R. A., and Sajtos, L., "Measuring Consumer Interactivity in Response to Campaigns Coupling Mobile and Television Media," *Journal of Advertising Research* 48, no. 3 (2008): 375–91 and Davis, R. A., and Yung, D., "Understanding the Interactivity Between Television and Mobile Commerce," *Communications of the ACM* July 48, no. 7 (2005): 103–105.

Fourth, the social media brand is inextricably linked to social media community, defined by CCE = Content, Community, Exchange. To drive interactivity and deep engagement focus on building great content, strong community and hence, exchange or the life blood of the social media brand value will flow.

Finally, change Daily. The social media brand is continuously evolving and constructed by the community and its stakeholders. Once those customers get control, they will constantly work as a team to make your brand relevant to the community. So, listen and learn.

Let's now move on, from exploration to specifics! In the following chapters I am going to focus on the *5-Sources Model*. To help interpret the importance and practical application of the approach to your brand, I am going to use real customers to explain how they view the applications. Remember the key: successful social media branding starts with listening to the customers and community.

CHAPTER 3

Source 1: Functional Social Media Brand

While experiencing and sharing your brand in social media such as Facebook or Twitter, customers tend to recognize its benefits, particularly in terms of service functionality. Customers come into contact with the brand to solve problems, send inquires or search for information. Customers also expect your brand to be convenient, accessible, and responsive to their needs.

> **Functional-Source**
>
> What is the role of the brand in the enablement of customer objectives?

They would like to evaluate offers before making a purchase decision, and that appears to be the essential part of its consumption in social media. Additionally, customers are interested in getting access to a brand's special deals and giveaways.

Problem Solving, Information Search, and Feedback

Social media is a great place for customer-to-customer help as it is consistent with the meaning and direction of the community. I think that this is a really powerful solution for small businesses. They are often criticized for the lack of manpower and support in servicing customers who have problems. Social media is a way for service to be brand related: linked to your customers and community. You never know: solving customers' problems and providing them good service may actually translate into positive word of mouth[1].

For example, Xero Live http://www.xero.com/ is a "software service platform" for accounting. Xero uses Twitter, Facebook, and LinkedIn to allow their customers to provide feedback on the service; problems are often resolved through these channels by Xero staff but most often by other Xero customers who have faced similar problems.

Customers consider social media as a platform for addressing their problems when other communication channels such as emails or phones are unavailable, inconvenient or time and/or money consuming. Occasionally many customers contact, for example, banks or Internet providers via Facebook and Twitter to solve emerging problems. Interestingly, customers' stories about their memorable experiences with brands often refer to functionality and particularly to problem solving.

It is really interesting how one customer said when getting help for their pets from the Vet:

> "One day I tweeted to my vet and I said: Look, I'm little worried about my dog, he has fleas once again, what would you recommend? And they just tweeted me back: try one course of prednisone. I would have usually had to call to the vet or gone down the road and be charged for this information. As it was—I just was sitting at my desk tweeting to my vet."

This example suggests that social media helps customers to reduce the amount they would normally pay for a service and allows them to do something that would have not been part of their online activities before Facebook or Twitter.

Value the Time of Customers

When customers were asked in what case they would contact a service using social media, many of them agreed that scheduling an appointment

---

[1] *See* for example Brown, Jo., Broderick, A.J., and Lee, N., "Word of Mouth Communication Within Online Communities: Conceptualizing the Online Social Network," *Journal of Interactive Marketing* 21, no. 3, pp. 2–20 (2007).

or sending inquires would be the case. As this customer reinforced that their time is valuable and often the need to do something is not conveniently matched with opening hours. Now customers want to engage with your brand *now*! Satisfying the need for convenience as well as impulse purchase behavior:

> "I don't have time to go to the branch. If I have a question I can chat with them via online consultant. And sometimes it's not a business hour. You know before social media the bank sent you a letter or insurance companies, for example. Now if I have a question regarding policy I can send them a tweet. And they would respond back to me. I have a car, a question regarding an accident I can send to my consultant as a tweet. Before social media there were no such things. You had to wait. Now you just go online and it's instant."

Nevertheless, some customers state that their concerns about privacy issues stop them from using social media for communicating, for example, with banks or other financial institutions. One customer explained when talking about banking online that there is a perceived lack of trust. As a small business owner it is important to think about how the customers perceived risk can be reduce and trust increased in the security of social media communication:

> "Neither would I 'like' my bank's Facebook page. Before I lived in the US, I probably would have. I have become more security conscious, especially here in Arizona. My name and other details are available, of course, but my bank? Not ready to do that yet. Life here is different."

Personal Life Context

In this regard, the degree to which customers are ready to use social media channels to contact a service provider depends on a customers' personal life context. For instance, the customer would not contact or show any relationship with a bank because of safety reasons. After moving to the USA, she started caring more about her own personal safety, which is contrary to her previous life in New Zealand. So, the personal context of the USA vs. New Zealand has a dramatic effect on her perceptions of risk. This does suggest that in social media, you just can't treat all your customers as one big mass of a community.

However, in contrast, some customers recognize the benefits of being involved with such services as banks and insurance companies in social media. Often these brands have developed their social media brand to create greater levels of trust. In the strategy described by this customer, the service provided a fee benefit for engaging through social media. As a small business owner, you will need to think about how you might incentivize your customers to engage with your social media brand:

> "With some companies you would never be engaged online, like a pharmacy. You have to go to a pharmacy. But insurance companies or your bank you would. And it is my choice, I do not use branches, and I never go back to the branch—they charge me a fee."

Problems Create Engagement

Interestingly, customers may never contact your brand in social media until certain problems occur. Maybe they see social media as being like a megaphone through which they will broadcast their problems with your brand. Customers start engaging with a brand when they experience some problems with a service provider. One customer pointed out this fact based upon their experience of a community attached to particular social media brands. It is quite clear that the opportunity to gripe about your brand is a way to create engagement and then conversation. For the small business owner it tells us to actually encourage our customers to have problems and share them to the world:

> "I'm almost prepared to bet that a lot of the companies that people follow; they did so 6 months, a year, 2 years ago. They've never looked at that Facebook site since, but because they have not bothered to go in and unlike . . . a page, it is just there, and it becomes part of the stats, I guess. Unless they have a problem, in which case they are all too quick on there and gripe about your brand."

From a customer's perspective, the possibility of problem solving is very high on the list of priorities relating to a service's functions in social media. The notion that a service should provide customers with regularly updated information has also become apparent. This brings together the idea of useful tips and information, new knowledge and the possibility to learn something new about a service offering. It can be suggested that a need for regularly updated information or useful advice is one of the reasons why customers engage with services within social media. This requires a shift away from the traditional way of talking or even shouting at your customers with advertising. It is a move toward thinking about the brand in social media as something useful. A tool that engages the customer to do something in a very functional way.

One customer brought forward a really important point here when talking about a newspaper social media brand. It had become like a service channel and enhanced the service experience component of the brand. It would have been difficult to predict that the new role for a newspaper brand is as a function tool in social media. For small business owners with products, this is a great way to enhance the intangible experience of their offline physical offering, online:

> "I get notifications from NZ Herald daily, because I want to be updated about national and world news. I also follow God Zone, from where I can learn changes in immigration policies and find other interesting facts about New Zealand. I Like Sal's NY Pizza just because in my opinion it is the best pizza I've ever had."

Emotions Create Following

Thinking further about following and engagement in social it is argued that the functional activities need to be justified and explicit. To move from simple following to engagement it is ideal that functionality is married to emotion. A simple example of this is related to why people regularly check Facebook? This is emphasized in the following customer vignette. But in many ways people regular check, which is a functional action, because of the need for hedonic engagement. Emotion is hedonic.

Why? Possibly they are in a state of boredom and they use the functional activity as a pathway to alleviate the mundane through emotion. Emotion could also relate to themselves because boredom itself is an internal cognitive state. Hence, it requires a self-directed solution:

> "I don't think that I would go and check business pages on a regular basis until I have a reason to. I'd rather spend my time checking news items, new tech coming up, something which adds to my informational level on any particular area. So I don't go and source a business page without reasons."

Additionally, there is a link between the need for information and the customers' personal context. Sometimes customers are forced by circumstances, such as a new geographical location or professional duties, to get involved with brands in social media. For example, one customer explained when talking about Airlines in that they engage depending on their sense of isolation or connection to their home location:

> "I used to be reading the Air New Zealand page, but I have unsubscribed one year ago. It always depends on where I am in the world now; it dictates which business pages I follow."

Engagement Through Learning Experiences

Customers often connect the need for information with the possibility of learning something new about a service. This may explain why the absence of any kind of expected information is likely to affect customers' service experiences. In other words, if you would like to have more engagement it is important your brand in the first interaction provides a learning experience linked to your brand. Don't just flash your logo or some special offer. Try and give those first time customers content that creates that stickability:

> "Often there is a campaign with a "like us." on Facebook button, and then people get to the Facebook page and they are like "what the hell." there is nothing here to recognize that. I have come to the Facebook page, and I want to learn more about it."

The feedback from customers also reveals that some customers are willing to provide brands with feedback regarding service quality using social media channels. *5-Sources Model* shows that customers use social media to publically express what they think about service quality, initiatives or even advertising campaigns. Social media for some brands has become like a constant test bed for ideas and innovation. As one customer strongly argued, social media helps them with the community cocreate campaigns with special relevance to the particular markets:

> "When they launched the Rico [Air NZ] campaign I was very vocal and particularly scathing in my critique of the campaign . . . I felt strongly that it undermined your brand significantly and could alienate the American market."

Prompt Action

The feedback from customers shows that in social media, customers expect prompt actions from a service provider in response to their emerging requirements. Customers point to social media as a short cut to address their emerging needs and to get a quick reply from your brand. One customer talked about the velocity of Twitter. Often it is that case that when you want an answer quickly; don't call. Go on social media:

> "I remember we were after a ticket, I think that was the New Zealand Open. So it was like last minute tickets available and my friend was after those tickets for us. And he communicated with that person from the New Zealand Open on Twitter. And he got replies like straight away, which for me was quite spectacular. We did not actually get what we wanted. But just the fact that they got back to us very quickly via Twitter, it was quite good."

This really brings forward an important question about service. Why are your service personnel on the phone at the bottleneck? It seems fair to suggest that social media impacts to a certain extent on customers' expectations concerning service functionality. How can it not? Other customers are really willing to help. For your brand it is important to shift toward the expectation that help needs to arrive through social media. It has become an expectation of your community. But, also realize that if you invest in that prompt action it enhances the learning experience of the community. Your content becomes a customer-based resource and can be deployed in the future. You may even find that prompt action resides in the velocity of the community-based response.

Convenience and Accessibility

From the customers' point of view, contacting brands via social media is more convenient than making phone calls or sending inquiries using websites. In this respect, consumption practices depend on how easily they can access the required information or reach the company's experts. In some cases customers prefer engagement with businesses within social media rather than phone calls or offline meetings, as this type of communication suits their life style more. I think that a large part of the momentum toward this model is being driven by the power of the Smartphone. It puts customers right in control because convenience is context based.

As one customer strongly suggested about the hassle of traditional methods. The way to move toward satisfying instant impulses that are intimately tied to their function objective:

> "Now the only thing that annoys you is when you do have to speak to someone and you're put on hold for five minutes before you get through to an operator, but so all those sort of service things I'd much prefer to actually do it online. You feel a lot more in control in a situation like that. I follow Air New Zealand on my Twitter. And they tweet something like, ok, hurry up, let's grab a deal. They just probably put two lines, but that is what makes me open their pages. I don't want to spend a lot of time going through the page, I want instant information so this information has to be there for me, and otherwise I will not be interested."

The enhancement of this type of engagement means that from a customer perspective, social media makes their communications with your brand more convenient and accessible.

Knowledge

The attributes of functional consumption seem to be related with each other. Customers use your brand's social media channels to not only evaluate offers and get an idea about a service provider, but also to gain tacit knowledge through personal experiences before making a purchase decision. Contrary to expectations, being present in a brand's social media channel does not imply a purchase intention. To be engaged with a brand and purchase from your brand are two different stories in the social media context. For example, as one customer argued:

> "Personally I do not choose brands or follow products just because they advertise on social media. I believe I don't put so much pressure on liking pages—it's not a big deal. Your purchasing decision may depend on deals which are going on, on easy access to information, interaction with a company, but I'm not sure that there is a link closely related to purchasing."

I like to think about my own personal experiences with Woodhill Mountain Bike Park. For me social media is about being up-to-date and to show to my community that I am a cool and rugged mountain biker. Yes, I admit it. My transactional activity is always offline. That is not to say though that if the right purchase related content was offered through social media, I would not consider it. But again, for this brand it would lead me offline. But it is also important to acknowledge that for some customers social media is likely to be a key factor in making a purchase decision.

Regardless of purchase intention, customers would like to get knowledge about a service provider and its service offering. Many customers consider social media as a tool for researching a brand. It is very interesting how this customer liked to see how the brand engaged with other customers. It is a bit like being a voyeur and for them it is an important component of deciding whether to like, engage, and even transaction:

> "Lost, because before I do anything I always look at people on Facebook or Twitter, to see what they are about, I always check their web page, if they didn't have Facebook, I wouldn't be able to see how they interact with people. As an example, with a car

mechanic, I want to know what is going on with this car mechanic before I go there. It's a way for us, as customers, to research the product, to research a coffee place before we go there."

Rewards

It comes as no surprise that often the customers' interest in businesses within social media is dominated by a need to have access to a brand's specials, giveaways, and gifts. This theme has been identified as rewards. In exchange for giveaways or discounts, customers are willing to participate in brand activities such as contests and opinion polls. For example, like this customer, it is a great way to get likes:

"I only 'like' what I actually like except if there is a good prize in it. If the company announces a contest via the app, I would definitely read it and depending on what it is I may participate, especially if there is a reward."

The findings also show that for some customers, possible rewards are the only reason they engage with a brand in social media as this customer explains:

"Seven days before the event we want to go to, I have checked out their [*Essenze Home Decor] Twitter page, LinkedIn page, what people say about it and their Facebook page as Dee (*wife) said to me "a contest is going on there." So I wrote a slogan and won a double pass to the event. That's the whole deal—you go there for a reason."

It is important to understand that the rewards process may also be a bit like playing a game for the community. The key question for your brand is whether you have developed a good enough game. What is the plot? Are there any levels and what point does the game end? That must be a novel idea for rewards and incentives in that it is more than just the offer but rather the hedonic experience of gameplay:

"I have a friend who follows every brand just for the sake of the freebies and whatever they're giving away. So he's constantly participating in all these contests to win something. He's doing it all the time. So it's like a game for him."

Engagement with brands in social media enables customers to stay informed about a company's deals and giveaways and participate in brand activities as soon as they become available on Facebook or Twitter. Interestingly, the findings show that such reward-focused communications with brands may lead to the beginning of a new relationship as one customer pointed out. Like most great deals, it helps customers move toward new phases of engagement:

"One of the pages I follow offered $99 headshots for a specific period. I took advantage of the offer and am delighted with the results. This means that I will take more notice of that page's updates in the future."

Closing Thoughts on the Functional Brand

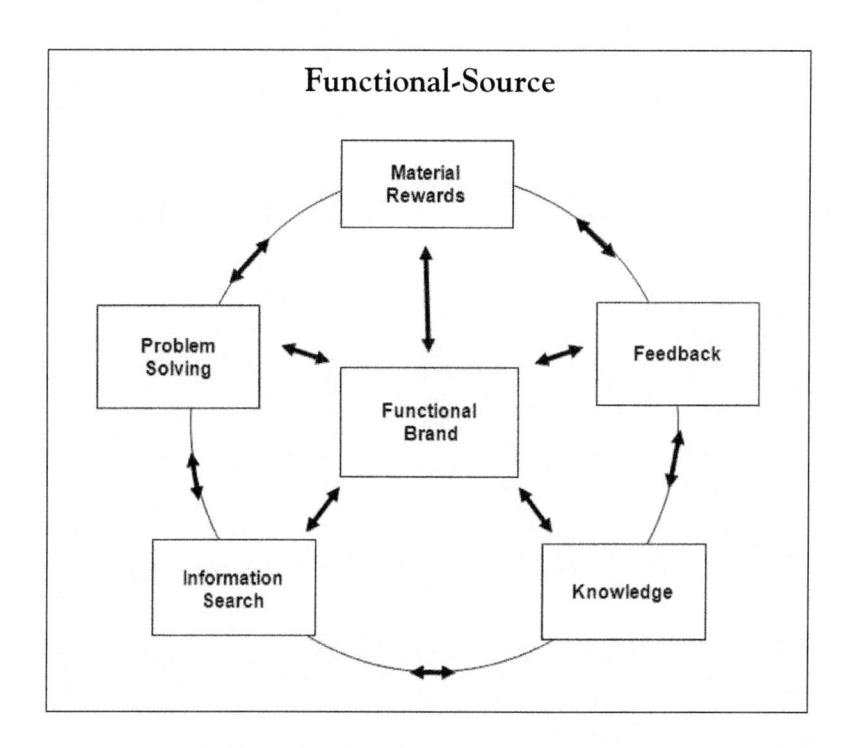

The *5-Sources Model* plays a key role in the customers' functional needs for problem solving, information search, providing feedback, access to deals and rewards, and overall for the evaluation of offers.

Engage in Problem Solving, Information Search, and Providing Feedback

What becomes evident is that customers use a brand's social media channels as a short cut to address their needs when traditional communication channels are unavailable, inconvenient or time and money consuming. Customers engage with the community because they want something that cannot be found in other market spaces. Hence, they seek the brand on Facebook and Twitter as a type of quality specific resource that will satisfy their demand and determines the customers' relationships with your brand.

Engage in Prompt Action, Convenience, and Accessibility

Interestingly, the consumption stories regarding brand experiences in social media often reflect the customers' need for timesaving solutions. Orientation toward time has been suggested as a powerful variable for better understanding the nature of customers' preferences and experiences. In this *5-Sources Model* the customers give emphasis to quick-fix solutions to emerging problems. They also refer to convenient and accessible brand experiences and the responsiveness of a service provider. However, in the context of social media, the ability to get the required information in time or to address problems as soon as they occur are associated with tangible benefits. It appears that social media is capable of implementing higher-order tasks such as a) cost and time effectiveness; b) reducing stress caused by problems, and c) better control of a situation by using a brand's proximity.

Consumption practices in social media are contextualized by the customers' personal situations and shaped through the context-specific ways in which they encounter and interact with a service provider. It can be suggested that the way customers experience a service is to a great extent formed by aspects that constitute customer situations. For example, physical surroundings might dictate how a service is consumed in social media. This situational dependency of consumption is shown in the *5-Sources Model* how customers use, for example, bank services.

Provide Knowledge to Drive Engagement

Functional brand consumption may have temporary arrangements based upon the customers' current situation and goals. For example, some services, particularly immigration, travel, and media are used to get knowledge about a new country. In this case, a brand's social media channels serve as an informational tool. Geographical location often dictates what brands are followed on Facebook and Twitter. Furthermore, from the customers' perspective, the possibility to learn something new or to advance their existing knowledge provides the impulse for engagement with a brand.

Having said that consumption experiences in social media are shaped by a variety of situations, it is important to look at them through the customers' concrete life contexts or life projects. For instance, a brand's social media channels are often used for learning or searching for information out of a sense of professional duty. The *5-Sources Model* proposes that customers follow brands in social media to track competitors' activities or get market knowledge and insights. This finding is supported by those who view their life projects as the construction and maintenance of key life roles and identities, for example, being a responsible employee.

Create the Game of Rewards to Provide Momentum for Engagement

The customers' communication with brands in social media is triggered by their intention to have access to a brand's deals and giveaways. This is the most common determinant of the customers' engagement with a brand and often the only one. Additionally, it is also important to note that there is an interrelation between how customers use social media channels to fulfill their utilitarian brand-related needs and the nature of brands. For instance, some customers may not contact financial services like banks or insurance companies for anything specific because of privacy issues.

However, they are likely to consider using social media for making an appointment or getting access to deals or giveaways. One of the *5-Sources Model*'s contributions is that social media changes not only the status of the customer in brand-relationships, but your brands as well. Brands assume a variety of roles and tasks in social media; they serve as information desks, emergency services, and a reception area, which are anchored in customer needs and situations.

CHAPTER 4

Source 2: Emotional Social Media Brand

The second source of social media brand is the customers' emotional connection to a brand and their need for enjoyable emotional experiences. These types of experiences are termed hedonic, meaning, that are engaged in by a customer and community for their own internal reasons. Often it is called the opposite of functional. In other words: for no other reason except for the enjoyment of the action itself.

Source 2 argues that customers communicate with brands in social media to alleviate personal problems or situations, to feel privileged and recognized by a brand, and to find fantasy and curiosity in brand experiences.

> **Emotional-Source**
>
> What is the role of the brand in customer acknowledgement?

Enjoyment

The *5-Sources Model* shows that the central idea of emotional brand consumption is an experience that provides the element of enjoyment. When customers were asked to about images that reflect their experiences with brands in social media they often chose those that represent happiness. For example, one customer chose a picture with a rock musician performing on stage in front of a large audience accompanied by the comment:

> "This is what you feel when you open their application [*Air New Zealand mobile application]. It is sooo good."

There is a fine line between the social, emotional, and self-oriented aspects of brand consumption. For example, the enjoyment from being involved in the cocreation of service offerings also enhances hedonic experiences. I was surprised by one customer's strong views that created the basis for learning and engagement:

> "Like yesterday I commented on a pull when somebody asked if LinkedIn should have an instant messenger. That's a new feature, I had a quite few things to say, I got engaged, I started going back to this page to check—there is so much for learning . . . And that is the value, value of information. I have my viewpoint, but that's one viewpoint. When 47 other viewpoints are coming at me—it got me."

As illustrated, the engagement with other community members can be seen as another source of enjoyment. As one customer who talked about the enjoyment when your community likes your comments making them feel like a superstar. It is like basking the glory of the brand and the community:

> "A couple of times actually with George FM, for example, and that's the thing. The biggest pleasure is when somebody likes your comments, somebody you don't know. And then if somebody liked it and especially like 5 or 6 people liked that comment you sort of feel like a superstar straight away."

Being Entertaining

Customers build relationships with brands in social media because it enhances the hedonic experience of enjoyment and entertainment. Customers appreciate experiences that provide the elements of entertainment and a touch of humor. I think that is why people like animals and in particular cats. I had to laugh the other day when I saw a post through Facebook on cat selfies, lol. For your brand, honestly ask whether it is funny and entertaining. Does it need to be?

"Like the Old Spice ads on YouTube . . . They're really funny, so it has to be something that I kind of engage with or find funny or compelling first and then your brand will literally get brand association by creating something that is like that. I'm not likely to wade through something that is instructional or self-serving."

Interestingly, some customers view online engagement with a brand, such as posting and commenting, as fun activities:

"If it was Whittaker's [*NZ chocolate brand], I'd say I love your product."

As customers argue that it is important that this posting and communication entertainment and regular. Otherwise, customers will slip into a cognitive state of boredom. If this is not alleviated that this could result in the negative consequence of disengagement and dysfunction;

"If I follow New World and they don't have a post at least once a week, I'm going to get really bored really quickly with them. And then if they do end up putting up a post and it's something that I find completely boring, or irrelevant to me, chances are I'll go off and get rid of them. I've done that a few times with companies."

Customers suggest that emotions created through engaging with consumption events may enhance the customers' hedonic experience and bring about a positive reaction to your brand. At the same time, a lack of enjoyable or entertaining experiences may result in weak customer-brand relationships.

Problem Alleviation

Emotion is also related to the alleviation of personal problems or a difficult situation. Because customers are situated in concrete every day contexts, the way they consume a brand does not just reflect these contexts. Their consumption is also formed by these contexts and situations.

Remember the customer who immigrated to the USA a long time ago stated that her connections with NZ Herald or Air New Zealand social media brands through Facebook helped her to feel emotionally close to her birth country. In this respect, your brand acts as a proxy to support the customers' gaps and insecurities in their personal life.

For others, connections with brands and others via social media help to overcome personal obstacles. For instance, one customer who runs his own construction company emphasizes that the necessity to go social media brands made him more confident and conversational:

> "I was afraid of becoming a part of a community; I was not interactive, but not anymore. I decided to start interacting to become a part of it and I'm stepping out of my comfort zone, because I'm confident about our business, I'm happy I can be a part of a community."

This indicates that the customers' relationship with a brand evolves out of a variety of emotional experiences in social media and some of these are deeply rooted in personality traits or personal circumstances. It is important for you to understand the underlying psychology of your customers. We have talked about the thought leading pivotals. But what about the hidden mass of customers who don't talk. Their views and engagement is vital. How are you going to motivate them to engage? One aspect of technology that can be leveraged in social media is that it is indirect and in many ways anonymous. Online customers will exhibit different behaviors compared to offline. Create the opportunities for them to do that with your social media brand.

Privilege

The *5-Sources Model* shows that customers tend to believe that their relationship with a brand can create some sort of personal advantage. It fosters feelings of being privileged and recognized by a brand. These emotional experiences make brands meaningful and tangible. Hence, the customer is transformed from being an invisible user, to a visible individual. Taking into account that social media presupposes a dialogue between brands and customers, the one-way old-fashioned approach bears little relationship to customers' needs. It makes customers feel invisible. The key question for your brand is: how does my social media brand engagement create a community of privilege and acknowledgment of the individual? Social media brands that are locked into traditional marketing communications and *shouting* at their customers will echo what this customer has experienced:

> "Less Meals, they don't do well. Their Twitter feed is one—for Less Meals worldwide. So if you tweet them, they don't respond. They don't retweet even if you have got something really interesting to say."

Privilege and recognition are distinctive features of brand consumption in social media and they cannot be ignored. These elements tend to be particularly meaningful in understanding relational aspects of consumption.

Fantasy

A need for an experience that provides some elements of fantasy or escapism has been identified as one of the emotional attributes of consumption. It can be suggested that consumption practices are motivated by customers' intending to find experiences, which on the one hand, serve as the opposite of reality and on the other hand reflect their desired reality. For example, as this customer argues:

> "Virtual fashion space can be very captivating, and sometimes takes me away from reality."

It seems logical to suggest that using some form of escapism in branding services can create emotional experiences for customers by reflecting their aspirations.

Curiosity

Customers' involvement with a brand often begins with curiosity and is fuelled by experiences and the knowledge that they develop through subsequent interactivity with a brand. The proximity of brands and customers within social media has turned brand affiliations into an interactive showroom, freely available and without time and location constraints. As a result, customers are motivated to research and explore brands, often just out of curiosity:

> "I've got a nut allergy and a beautiful Anzac recipe was posted up on one of the chefs I follow. And I asked a question, do I need to substitute it with more flour to make it more balanced and she [*a chef] got back straight away and said . . .

If a brand arouses curiosity, it is likely that there will be repeat consumption, as the customer wants to maintain a connection and learn from personal experiences about the brands evolution:

> "Like Pinterest, 11 million people on it, it's the fastest growing network ever. But if someone asks me' Hey, do you really need to use Pinterest?—No, I don't think so. 'I don't have business there, I don't make many of it, it's curiosity and knowledge, and I want to know what this is. That's what keeps me going back and keeping engaged with Pinterest. It's the whole thing about—there might be something about it, and the only way is to go and find out."

In the context of social media, curiosity is a challenge for brands and a driver of consumption, as there is always something customers want to find out. That is why with your social media brand it is important to create platforms of conversation. This helps customers to continually be in that state of curiosity and learning. Possibly, this will be another factor that will drive the engagement toward your brand.

Closing Thoughts on the Emotional Brand

The *5-Sources Model* identified the need for enjoyment and entertainment in brand experiences. Customers have migrated from the production of services to the production of experiences and consequently, in social media, a primary experience of value is emotion.

Emotional-Source

```
                    Curiosity ←→ Enjoyment
                   ↙         ↘  ↙         ↘
          Fantasy ←→    Emotional Brand    ←→ Entertainment
                   ↖         ↗  ↖         ↗
              Privilege/                Problem
              Recognition              Alleviation
```

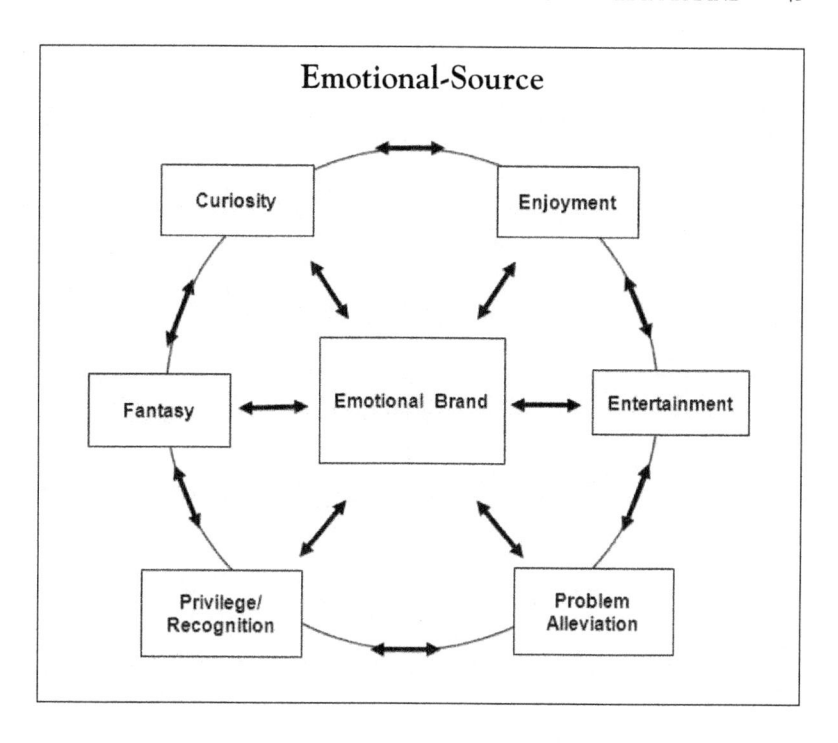

Customers are looking for brand experiences that provide elements of fantasy, curiosity, make them feel privileged and help to alleviate personal problems.

Engagement Through Enjoyment and Entertainment

The *5-Sources Model* recognizes that customers build relationships with brands in social media because it enhances their experience of enjoyment and creates some sort of personal advantage. The *5-Sources Model* shows that enjoyment evolve from their conversations with brands and other customers as well as from the customers' participation in the development of the service offerings.

In this light, cocreation enhances the experience of enjoyment. Customers derive emotional benefits from planning, creating, enjoying, and remembering the experience in close cooperation with other cocustomers. Customers emphasize that the degree to which they are willing to participate in a brand activities, to some extent, depends on your brand's contents and communication style. The *5-Sources Model* shows that customers are likely to avoid self-contained, dry, and direct communications that push hard for sales. Instead, customers have a need for experiences that provide elements of fun, humor, entertainment, and grass roots communications, either with a brand or other customers.

Problem Alleviation Creates Engagement

Here again, the importance of concrete customer situations in which emotional brand experiences are developed. Customers use brand affiliations as both recreational and treatment facilities, for example to deal with homesickness. For example, *5-Sources Model* of the customers' involvement with some companies illustrates that a brand acts as a proxy to plug the gaps in their personal lives. Customers also use brand communities to overcome their insecurities about themselves. In this regard, engagement with a brand and other customers helps to develop confidence in their personal skills and abilities.

A relationship that derives from a personal situation may result in an emotional connection with a brand. In support of this, some see building relationships with customers as the establishment of the experience of the brands emotion. This emotion goes well beyond functional objectives but describes the love between brand and customer. In some cases, it may also exhibit almost "spiritual" properties. For example, in the case of the fandom of sports teams.

Engagement Through Fantasy

The *5-Sources Model* promotes the important of fantasy as an element of emotional consumption. In the context of social media, fantasy has the dual role of offering a form of escapism and aspirations. The visualization and personalization of a desired reality, particularly in relation to travel and fashion industries, creates emotional ties between brands and customers. One of the outcomes of emotional experiences is the enjoyment customers get out of the anticipation of pleasure as they plan or envisage the coming event.

Curiosity Creates Learning and Engagement

Curiosity is another element of emotional brand consumption. Even though curiosity is not unique to a brand, in the context of social media it helps to enrich the conversation between customers and brands and is consequently a worthwhile element when the interactive nature of consumption is taken into account. It creates opportunities for repeat consumption. In some cases a dialogue between brands and customers begins with curiosity; customers undertake actions to satisfy their need to uncover your brand or to know more about it. The importance of fantasy and curiosity in service-related consumption practices is supported by the assumption that service experiences should be pertinent to the individual self. Ask yourself what do your customer desire in their inner brand fantasies?

Engagement is Part of Privilege and Recognition

The emotional connection is more than providing customers with enjoyable and entertaining experiences. Customers express their interest in personalized conversations that make them feel privileged and recognized by a brand. In the context of social media, customers expect brands to be responsive, conversational, and attentive. Customers want their brand-related activities to be noticeable and appreciated by a brand. Brand affiliation is like a portal for knowledge, emotions, and privilege. As a result, it is symbolic of the relationships formed by providing a sense of tangible reality. Personalized communications builds a bridge between all the identified consumption aspects and the scope of your branding activities.

ND# CHAPTER 5

Source 3: Self-Oriented Social Media Brand

The third source of social media brand relates to the customers' experiences and two strands of connection: the "self" concept (actual and ideal) and the social self. In this sense, customers express their interest in experiences that resonate with their life style. With their personal or professional goals or that help to facilitate and organize their daily activities.

> ### Self-Sourcing
> What is the role of the brand in the transformation of customer acknowledgment to actualization?

Overall, this is the customers' self-reflective perspective on consumption practices in social media. Consumption in social media is frequently motivated by the customers' needs in relation to self-actualization, self-perception, and self-branding.

Self-Actualization

Engagement among brands and customers and the community take many forms in social media and it encompasses a variety of aspects in which self-actualization holds a notable position in consumption practices. Customers search for self-actualization in their experiences with brands in social media. In other words, if brands hold the promise that the customers' individual needs will be met, they will engage.

For some customers social media present new opportunities to realize their potential through brand-related activities. In this regard, customers take a very active role, encouraged by a network-oriented medium . . .

"I'm nosy. I would definitely say that this engagement with businesses and with people in social media adds value to my life, definitely. And it adds value to my perception of value I can give other people. Years and years ago on the back of a bus was an ad saying—'listen to news on your way to work and you will be far more interesting person by the time you arrive.' I'm always knowledge taking, that is what I want to do. Customers value the possibility to express themselves and share their endeavors or ideas through brand communications. It enhances their feeling of self-worth and makes the experiences valuable."

Self-Relevance

Throughout feedback from customers, self-relevance has been identified as a common aspect of brand consumption among customers. Customers tend to engage with a brand if your brand's symbolic meanings are congruent with their sense of self. If customers perceive a brand's symbolic meanings as relevant to their personal values, interests, and beliefs they are likely to engage in consumption in social media. For example, it is interesting how one customer talked about the importance of the ethics related to a brand. The key question for your brand asks: what is it about your brand that is consistent with your customers' values, interests, and beliefs?

"Companies have to sit well with the customer so I'm very, very conscious of that. So I'll only like companies that I admire or who have the same ethical background that we have."

Self-relevance seems to be one of the key factors in consumption, since it creates a strong affiliation with a brand. One customer pointed out that she would divide all businesses into two groups, depending on consumption activities. Those that are deal oriented and those that are like me:

"I would divide all companies I follow on Facebook into two groups. First group consists of companies I joined by chance, who offered a good deal/price. Second one represents business I just like, which demonstrate my interests and hobbies."

The example illustrates that brand experiences could serve as a link to the customers' sense of self and, therefore, make these experiences tangible and meaningful. However, in a few cases, customers point to professional duties as the main drivers behind their engagement with brands in social media. One customer strongly supported the idea:

> "I do follow a lot of businesses because I like to keep an eye on what they do. I also follow general industry people and journalists. I would follow a business more out of a sense of professional duty than through compelling interests of my own to follow them."

Interestingly, the feedback from customers also indicates a specific social media effect. Customers often consider your brand's relevance to themselves. The sense of the belonging is a bit like being part of a club. It is important for you to understand what club your brand may represent to customers. If so, what defines membership and participation in the club?

> "One example would be Giapo; it's an ice cream shop in the town. It's a tiny—tiny little ice cream shop. I have never even been to his ice cream shop, but I know him, I know about his specials, I know when he is making new flavors, never met him, but he creates a feeling of like a little club, like Giapo club. And I don't even like ice cream."

The customer's brand preferences in social media are convertible, dynamic, and unstable. Your brand may fail in the self-relevancy dimension, but it still creates a connection with customers through interactivity and cocreation. However, in general, *5-Sources Model* reinforces the notion that customers search for brand experiences that resonate with their interests and values.

Self-Branding

Brands in social media contexts seem to provide customers with opportunities to create an identity that depends on their personal goals. Self-branding is characterized by customer's actions that are undertaken to build their social self-identity through different brand-activities, including brand endorsement and brand affiliations. Customers use social media experiences with brands for a multitude of reasons, including self-promotion. By publicly showing their affiliation with certain brands, customers on the one hand differentiate themselves from others, and on the other hand, indirectly give their followers a notion about the knowledge, expertise, skills, and interests they want to be associated with:

> "I only like to post maybe three to four times a week. If I found that other people found it interesting I'll repost it but I will take away the link to show where it came from. So it almost looks as if it's something that I magically found. And I try, also on my personal page, to like a lot of European pages, so that what I'm bringing through is something a little different. A different perspective, different culture, different ideas, different chefs . . . I think it's a unique selling point as well. I have to, I work for a company but also I mightn't work for them in two or three years' time. I think it's very important as a person to brand myself."

Self-branding also serves as a driver for engagement in brand cocreation activities, when customers take a role, for example, as product critics. Here as an example of how cocreation works in social media:

> "A couple of weeks ago I was approached by an ice cream brand which is starting up. Delicious stuff. And they said: "We would love you to try and if you like it, talk about it." They didn't say you must tweet about it or I didn't really feel obligated to blog about it or anything like that. But I tried their stuff and because I genuinely liked it, I tweeted about it."

Such customer experiences are noticed by others due to the network-oriented environment of social media. Therefore, consumption for self-branding to some extent contributes to the construction of a customer's social "self". If brands continue assigning the role of product tester or reviewer to customers, other community members will perceive this person as an expert in a field. In general, self-brand consumption creates ties with brands and makes the experiences meaningful for customers if their personal needs are satisfied.

Life Arrangements

The next aspect that emerged as a subcategory of self-oriented consumption is the customers' need for brand experiences that help to facilitate, optimize, and manage different daily tasks. New insights explain the internal logic that directs some consumption practices in social media. It is argued that the customers use the proximity of a brand in social media to get, for example, news updates or information when it is needed, or to address their personal inquires as soon as they occur.

In this regard, there is a link between the functional and self-oriented aspects of consumption as customers use a brand's social media applications as a tool that facilitates their daily activities. Many customers argued strongly for this idea:

> "Well, the coffee shop down the road here is Metro Coffee Shop. You tweet them and they will have the coffee ready when you arrive, instead of going in the queue."

> "I wake up in the morning and I check my tweets because I want to see what happens now on NZ Herald. I don't wait for the newspaper to arrive in my mailbox, I check my tweets first. It's how I get my information."

The idea of life arrangement is really important to your customers because their life is a social mechanism. Social media is seen to be that world. Helping to organize and facilitate:

> "The purpose of social medium is to create an exchange of value directly with one another. It's not business transactions."

At the same time customers think that social media reformulates, for example, how the people consume brands in their daily lives:

> "I see very few young people that will ever look at newspapers. If they do they might consume a little bit on their iPad and get it, but they're more likely to get onto an iPad and go to flip board. The only way they're hearing about things is because they're on the social media and people are talking about it within their peer

group. Then they'll go to check it out from that source. So normally the route is through peers."

Obviously, the integration of social media in customers' lives signifies a general shift in their consumption activities. The *5-Sources Model* illustrates that customer's need experiences that help manage daily tasks that are related to their personal or professional life. In this respect, the need to simplify or facilitate day-to-day activities serves as a driver of consumption in social media and adds overall value to a consumption process:

> "New Zealand's a very small country, in most business sectors you find the same people moving around within a sector. So you get the same ideas everywhere, and that may be good, but for a lot of things getting an external perspective or getting ideas from outside can deliver a lot of value."

Closing Thoughts on the Self-Oriented Brand

Social media brand consumption, regardless of context, is a dynamic and complex process, which is formed by the customers' social and personal determinants, including the notion of self.

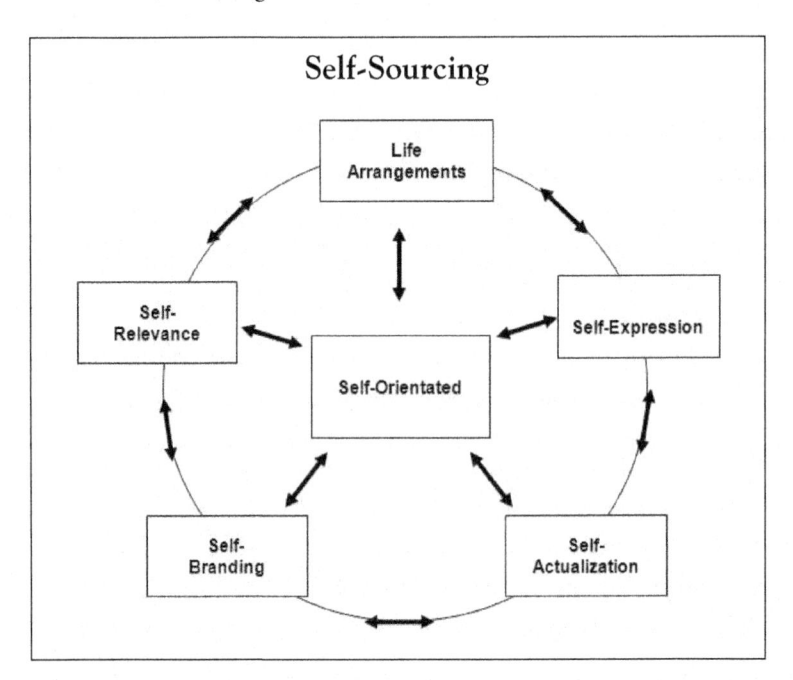

Self-Sourcing

- Life Arrangements
- Self-Expression
- Self-Actualization
- Self-Branding
- Self-Relevance
- Self-Orientated

Even though there is a generally accepted view that the self-concept is inherent in all consumption practices, the *5-Sources Model* produced some novel insights on how customers develop and realize their social roles and self-identities through experiences with brands in social media. In this light, the *5-Sources Model* identified self-actualization, self-expression, self-relevance, life arrangements, and self-branding as the attributes of self-oriented social media brand consumption.

Engagement Through Self-actualization, Self-expression, and Self-branding

Brands within a social media community are assigned to perform more than just instrumental functions directed toward customers' utilitarian needs. What seems to emerge is that customers use self-brand connections to construct and communicate their self-concepts. Customers take an active role in their relationships with brands, driven by a need to present their true or inner self to the outside world and to have others know them as they know themselves.

The relationships with brands are used firstly as a means of realizing personal goals, such as to be in the know or giving back to the community through sharing knowledge, networking, and building communities. Customers appreciate the possibility to express their own thoughts and ideas. Some customers emphasized that social media gives them courage to voice personal opinions. It helps customers feel a part of something tangible and real as an individual and as a part of the group. Hence, your brand experiences within social media have two strands of connection: to the self-concept (actual and ideal) and the social self.

Customers also tend to use the symbolic meanings of brands to enhance their social identities through brand endorsement and brand-related activities. Customers voluntarily share their self-brand connections on Facebook and Twitter to: a) show which brand communities they belong to, which positively contributes to the construction of the social self, and b) give others a notion of their interests, knowledge, and professional skills. It is argued that the customer often relies upon the information from the community about products and services to form their own congruent self-image.

Some customers consider brand affiliations in social media as a platform for self-branding. Being actively involved in engagement with brands and other people, customers build and raise their social profiles. The desired social image and the encouragement customers get from brands through, for example, offering to participate in the evaluation of new service initiatives or advertising campaigns, boosts their self-esteem and make them keep going with the assigned role of an expert in a field.

In this regard, the attention from other customers in the form of comments and likes also inspires their confidence in what they do in social media. The personal benefits provided through such engagement creates a sense of brand tangibility and as a result: repeat consumption.

Self-relevance Creates Engagement

Self-concept is constituted by a variety of self-related meanings, including a customer's goals, motives, and values which are viewed as characteristics of self-relevance. Engagement with brand affiliations in social media needs to be relevant to customers as symbols of their specific self-identities. For example, self-relevance determines what kind of brands customers follow in social media, the brands they are likely to engage with and endorse and the brands they tend to advocate.

There are different sources of self-relevance in a social media context. For instance, customers may engage with a brand motivated by professional duty. In this respect, a brand may be relevant to a customer as a symbol of responsible employee self-identity. At the general level, Facebook and Twitter serve as informational business channels where responsible employees can get insights on any industry they are interested in, regardless of their occupations.

Some customers are motivated by higher-order tasks, such as self-actualization. At this point, the source of personal relevance is intrinsic and the value of self-brand connections evolves from the realization of customers' potential and personal goals. Obviously, customers are likely to get involved with brands that fit well with their personal interests and life style. Personal interest is a precondition for the strong emotions that trigger customer coproduction and influence of the outcome.

Life context can also be considered as another source of personal relevance. In some cases, customers get involved with brands after being motivated by a concrete situation, for example, traveling or studying overseas. In this regard, a new situation produces a different set of goals, which may change as soon as the situation changes. Moreover, social media creates such consumption situations where the self-relevance aspect can be negotiated. For instance, customers may perform activities that are associated with brands that are not personally relevant. More specifically, the customers' involvement with a brand may have temporary arrangements; some have been asked by friends or colleagues to like a brand and others have been motivated by sales promotions or available giveaways.

The *5-Sources Model* also identified that the network-oriented nature of social media may motivate customers to join brand affiliations even if there is no direct link between a brand's characteristics and a sense of self-relevance. The example of an ice cream shop illustrates that customers participate in brand communities not because they like a product or a service, but because they like the feeling of being a part of a community. However, it seems logical to suggest that social media represents a sort of situational source of self-relevance, which includes a wide variety of specific stimuli, cues, and contingencies in a customer's immediate environment.

Engagement Through Life Arrangements

The feedback from customers points to the customers' need for brand experiences that help to facilitate and organize day-to-day tasks. Such consumption practices have been identified in relation to media, sport, telecommunication, travel and leisure services. What is being witnessed here is that customers tend to organize regular consumption activities on a base of social media. It came as no surprise that customers prefer getting news on Twitter, since it meets their need for instant information. Contacting banks, vet clinics, or a car mechanic via Facebook or Twitter is also accepted as a common practice in social media.

From the customers' perspective, it helps them to 1) have brand experiences that suit their personal schedules, and 2) effectively organize daily tasks, from getting news updates to making appointments. In this respect, customers tend to ascribe organizing properties to social media. It seems logical to assume that by effectively managing their daily activities (including brand-related), customers take on the role of technologically advanced, self-disciplined and organized individuals, which reinforces their sense of self. The benefits resulting from such brand engagement presumably lead to repeat consumption and the development of a reference point for customers.

CHAPTER 6

Source 4: Personal (Social) Media Brand

The customers' need for sharing personal experiences and engagement with others characterize brand consumption in social media. The social dimension shows that customers use social media for experience exchange, community attachment, link building, and social engagement.

> **Social-sourcing**
>
> What is the role of the brand in the reality
> of a customers social interactions?

Experience Exchange

Customers use social media to share their personal brand experiences with others. In this light, customers are willing to broadcast their consumption activities and experiences not only for their own benefit and self-promotion, but also for the benefit of others. It is expected that customers would pay attention to what businesses their friends like or follow in social media. Some customers follow their friends' recommendations even if your brand is outside their personal or professional interests. But others are skeptical about the influence of social media WOM. The key question for your brand is what will help to drive the word of mouth"

"What Facebook is trying to sell is personal recommendations. They're always saying that a personal recommendation is the most powerful thing you can get, which is absolutely true, for a plumber or an electrician or anything like that. I just don't think it's quite as neat as Facebook think it is . . . To be honest I don't actually see a lot of people of my Facebook friends recommending companies, I don't think it happens, out of my friends it doesn't happen a lot, it might be different for other people."

Different attitudes toward friends' recommendations. Firstly, customers don't always tend to rely on friends' opinions, unless their friend is credible:

"Recommended by friend's means I probably have something for me there."

"You get to a point that if certain people send it to you, then you'll follow it, so it's the people that you align with or you think are credible."

Secondly, customers tend to test all recommendations on their relevance to their interests and values:

"I would see if a recommended page fits my interests, then check and make a final decision if it's interesting to follow or not."

"I wouldn't promote something for a friend if I didn't believe in the product, because that doesn't help them nor does it help me in my relationships."

Whereas there is no coherence on the role of friend recommendations in brand consumption, almost all customers are in agreement that public opinion plays an important role in a service evaluation. The next example clarifies this is the context of tourism services:

"We were leaving for Queenstown for a holiday. So I looked through holiday homes because I didn't want to live in a hotel. I want to stay in a house. I checked some business pages. . . I think nowadays it's not even about experiencing; you might not even have experiences with a company, but what other people say about it. If somebody has a really bad experience, and they put about it on a page and in the back of your mind you can think that what happened to this person might happen to me. Nowadays is about what other people think. It becomes really important."

While the idea concerning the impact of friends' recommendations on brand consumption is only partly supported by customers, the community knowledge produced by social media seems to play an essential role in consumption practices. Customers tend to share both negative and positive brand experiences for the benefits of others.

Community Attachment

Consumption activities can be oriented toward the customers' social need for getting engagement with other members of a social media community. In this light, the social dimension of consumption should be linked with your brand community. Customers feel a sense of community being involved in Facebook or Twitter brand affiliations, particularly revolving around brands. Customers articulate the importance of being able to engage with a brand community. This is mostly motivated by the notion that social media give the possibility to voice opinions and be heard. It is a bit like your customers want your brand, which was mute, to now have a voice:

> "It's important to belong to something. I don't know why it's necessarily social media, it's not like I have a lack of friends, and people are social creatures, right? We want to have a voice. That's why you want to be a part of community."

> "Internet gives you courage; it allows you to say anything you wouldn't normally say. And it also allows you to feel like you belong to people who don't know each other, but they feel a sense of community."

Interestingly, customers pointed toward the difficulty of building a community around a brand. At the same time they believe that a community should be seen as a pledge of support for your brand in social media...

"There are some New Zealand food brands that have done a great job building online communities, probably it's paid dividends for them in the sense that people might be a little bit more reluctant to speak badly about that brand on social, because they know that brand is actively engaged on social media and has represented themselves as a person or created a personality. So it feels like if you were to slag them off you would be slagging off a friend. I don't think people have got the same qualms about doing that to a bank or to a Telco."

The feedback from customers shows that the customers' communal brand experiences in social media often relate to communities that have emerged around product brands. The following example gives a notion about the customers' perception of what a community is about within a social media context:

"One example would be Giapo; it's an ice cream shop in the town. It's a tiny—tiny little ice cream shop. I have never even been to his ice cream shop, but I know him, I know about his specials, I know when he is making new flavors, never met him, but he creates a feeling of like a little club, like Giapo club. He has created this following, and the other day he is like "ok, I need feijoa leaves. Who's got feijoa leaves?" and everybody offered feijoa leaves and he got them for free. This way he has made a Twitter feels like they are a part of this endeavor he was doing. He has made contact with people; they are all now talking about this new ice cream he is making with these feijoas and leaves, which were donated."

Whatever the outcome, the key question here is: can a brand bring customers a sense of community and add value to consumption? Customers bond with brands in social media is shaped by their communal experiences.

Link Building

Link building and networking for professional or personal purposes seem to be an important part of consumption in social media. Customers appreciate the opportunities for developing new relationships through brand affiliations in social media but some customers are likely to limit their communal ties to social media. For example, when answering the question whether customers would like to personally meet people who follow the same brand in social media, some of them are in two minds about it:

> "I would meet people [*offline] who shared a political affiliation, but not someone who liked the same company."

However, at the general level, customers recognize the benefits of being engaged in a brand community, particularly in terms of link building and networking:

> "It's not as fast as face to face, it is not in real time, but there is definitely interaction on air, which you can call communication. And in terms of networking, yes, because you never know when your network is going to be important to what you are doing right now. There is one other thing I've understood in the past is that necessity builds the relationship before you need to rely on relationship. You have to be creating relationships that you can call on or be called on in the future. And by continuing communication again you are putting yourself in front of somebody. So when they ask the questions you become the picture in their mind."

The link between the customers' engagement in a brand community and their personal goals of self-actualization and self-branding is apparent. In this case, through participation in brand communities and networking, social connections between customers and brands add value not only to brand experiences, but to the customers' lives as well:

> "I would definitely say that this engagement with businesses and with people in social media adds value to my life, definitely. And it adds value to my perception of the value I can give to other people."

The relationship with brands through connections with others may also foster and support other emotions and activities. Your brand also plays a role in creating those links. The key question is how?

Social Engagement

The feedback from customers indicates that customers use brand communities in social media to get social engagement with other customers. The customers' communal experiences do not necessarily imply an attachment to a brand community or the intention to network. Furthermore, customers do not purposefully seek engagement with a brand. It is more likely that customers respond to your brand's activities if there is a promise of communication with others:

> "I do read comments with interest. The larger the number of comments, the more I like to read. What keeps me connected and keeping an eye on that site/page is the number of likes."

> "I wouldn't like to join a 'dead' page just because someone sent me an invitation. It should be in my areas of interest, but it also should work, make daily updates, create discussions, upload pictures, offer to take part in competitions with some rewards, keep me informed about new things."

Being involved with a brand in social media means that customers read and post comments, repost and retweet your brand's links and photos, ask questions, address personal problems, provide feedback, share experiences, and build networks. Often these consumption practices are motivated by the customers' need for socializing with other members of a social media community, which makes them feel as if they are a part of something tangible and real, as an individual and a part of the group.

Closing Thoughts on the Personal Brand

The *5-Sources Model* proposed that brand relationships in social media are also shaped by the customers' need for social experience, particularly for sharing knowledge, engagement with others, community attachment and link building.

Social-Sourcing

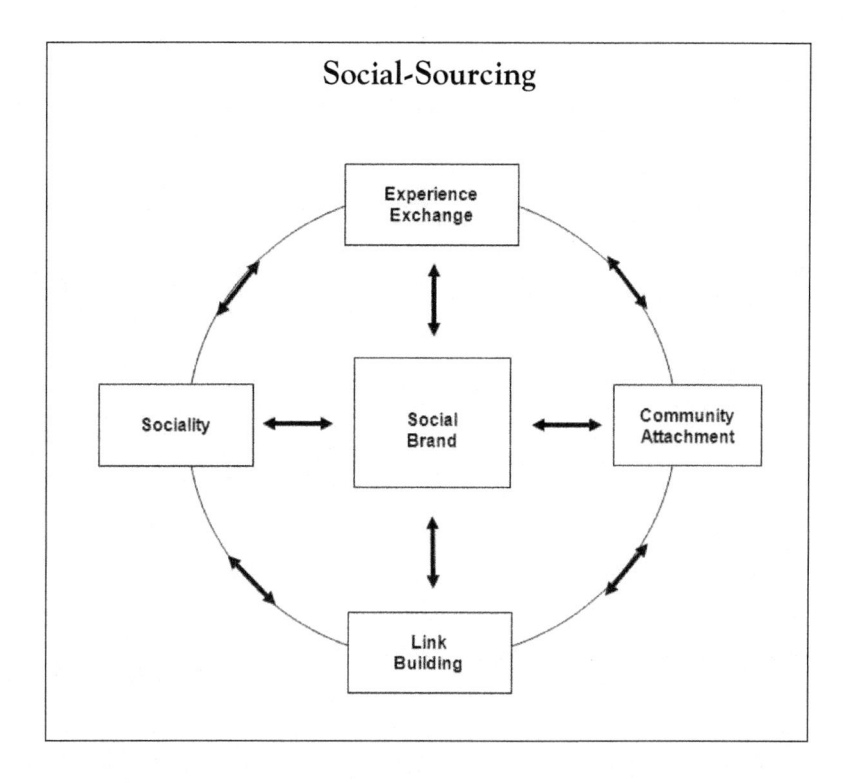

```
          Experience
          Exchange
              ↕
Sociality ↔ Social ↔ Community
            Brand     Attachment
              ↕
            Link
          Building
```

Customers want to know about and be part of what is happening in society, the need for community attachment is not a common theme. The customers expressed different views regarding the role of a community in brand consumption. Your brand relationship through connections with others fosters and supports emotions and enhances the sense of purpose and self-worth. It also enables them to focus on pivotal points of communication within their network of relationships. But this is not typical of all customers; some of them are more likely to be driven by utilitarian needs, for example, getting insights on a service provider through observing your brand community.

Experience exchange and engagement with others through engagement

The *5-Sources Model* demonstrates that customers are willing to share either positive or negative personal experiences for the benefit of others. They help to educate and to create some form of collective knowledge. The customers also tend to rely on their friends' opinions in the choice of services, such as a hotel, a restaurant, or a travel agency. Many of them are likely to put trust in the community knowledge produced by a social media community. Customers emphasize that prior to making a purchase decision; they prefer to assess the credibility of a brand via Facebook or Twitter.

The *5-Sources Model* shows that attention is paid not only to the quality of content, brand responsiveness and the regularity of information updates, but to the number of brand followers and their communication with brands as well. Contrary to the widely accepted belief that customers are interested in brands' contents rather than in numbers of brand likes and followers, the *5-Sources Model* shows that in a social media context, numbers give customers a notion of brand credibility.

Customers use brand affiliations in social media to get engagement with others. In a similar vein, online communities have become increasingly organic aggregate meeting-places, not focused around a brand but around practices (or "lifestyles") under which various discourses are negotiated. In this respect, what the customer reveals is that although a conversation between customers is often not directly related to a brand, the conversation is held within a brand community, which literally means that your brand gives customers a place to talk.

In this way a brand becomes meaningful and may bring customers a sense of community, even though this community has been generated by businesses and for business purposes. However, it should be mentioned that the need for social engagement with others is not a common theme, as a several customers did not show any interest in conversations with community members.

Engagement through attachment to community and link building

Online brand communities are usually guided by several factors, including the relationships between the person and the central consumption activity that they are engaging in and the actual social relationships of the online community itself. In this regard, the intensity and degree of customer involvement in a brand community depends, on the one hand, on the customer's sense of self and on the other hand, on the social bonds within the community.

Customers did manifest their intention to be a part of brand communities. For example, Air New Zealand, New World and Giapo communities on Facebook and Twitter. Communities revolving around product brands, brands need to provide convincing arguments for engagement, while having a liking for a product is a good enough reason for joining a brand community. More specifically, the customers gave a variety of reasons why they follow services on Facebook and Twitter, but they were mostly related to the customers' utilitarian needs.

The customers' involvement in a product-focused brand community is motivated more by their emotional attachment: I just like the product. This can be explained by the complex and intangible nature of services. The fact that your brand communities that have emerged in social media, are business focused, and sponsored by companies may also impact on the degree to which customers are willing to invest time and ideas and share their experiences with a community.

Online communities have no barriers to entry and exit, resulting in great freedom of movement for customers—one day they are in and the next day they are out. The shallow, transient nature of many online engagement results in weak social bonds and this indicates that online brand communities should be used selectively to support community needs because the online community on its own is not a community strategy.

The *5-Sources Model* shows that participation in service-oriented brand communities does not directly indicate a community attachment. However, it does provide social benefits such as networking and link building. For example, some customers expressed their interest in building new relationships with like-minded people. Online connections evolving from brand communities may develop further and go beyond the online context. However, customers are in agreement that to start developing, the relationship needs to be based on common personal or professional interests, not just on a liking for the same brand. The customers' need for social engagement with others and link building is supported by the assumption that there are two ways that brands can contribute to the relationships that customers experience in their daily life. The first type is brand and customer relationships, while the second is the links that customers develop with other customers around your brand that are viewed as brand communities.

CHAPTER 7

Source 5: Relational Social Media Brand

The *5-Sources Model* concludes with a discussion of the relational social media brand. Customers are engaged in personalized brand communications through interactivity and cocreation.

> ### Relational-Source
>
> What is the role of the brand in
> defining collective relationships?

In this context, personalized communication means a "human touch," which appears to be an important dimension of the relational aspect of consumption. Simply speaking, customers do not want to interact with a faceless organization. They would like to know the real people behind your brand. The customers' direct discourse with a brand and their cocreation activities form a bridge at the level of relational bonds. In this light relational bonds are identified as a) Fickle; b) Obliged; c) Preexisting; d) Emerged, and e) Casual.

Personalized Brand Communication

The *5-Sources Model* shows that customers expect brands to provide them with personalized communications. Moreover, customers want to establish close contact with brand representatives or experts in social media. What appears to take place in social media leads to the customers' greater expectations of a brand experience. Customers want to be able to have a conversation with a real person behind your brand, either a brand representative or an industry expert. For example, as this customer argues:

> "That's the thing with online; it's such an intimate space. It's sort of public, but at the same time it's one on ones. You don't really talk to the corporation any more you talk to the person who started it. If you have a person behind that brand page, and if you know that you're talking to somebody who is passionate about this business, I guess just having a human face for that page would be like a good start."

Social media enables a shorter distance between customers and brands, creating a notion that there is always someone who listens and can fix a problem:

> "People don't want to necessarily speak to the online community manager. They want to have a conversation about it [*bank mobile app] with the guy that built the app. I don't have time to go to the branch [* bank]. If I have a question I can chat with an online consultant. And sometimes it's not a business hour."

Brand experiences in social media by default hold the promise of a personalized conversation with brands. From a customer's perspective, brands become close and real in social media. This is supported by the customers' stories about communications with banks, airlines, and other service providers:

> "I like the fact that I can express my side as well. Like recently Vodafone did a poll on "if you were given extra broad band, what you would use it for?" It makes you feel like you're engaging in a business decision."

Customers expect brands to be in social media to continue the conversation with them online. They get disappointed when they can't develop and share this relationship with the community. It is like a sense of pride:

"The thing is that with companies that I like—they're not on Facebook. There is my hairdresser. They're amazing, these punk ladies in their 60s and they're so funky and so cool and I love talking to them, and I think they would be great on Facebook, but they're not. So I can't even like this company, to show people that I like them."

Personalized communication with a brand and the possibility of being engaged in brand life are two important elements of the relational aspect of consumption. It gives customers tactile experiences and could potentially add value to consumption by bringing them in to the ongoing process of brand cocreation.

Fickle Relational Bonds

Throughout the feedback from customers, four themes have been identified as a relational bond that customers form with brands in social media. One of the categories that emerged is "fickle relations," which appears to mean being unstable, unpredictable, and changing in accordance with a current stage of experience. Having the representation of all sorts of businesses along with information on them available in social media makes customers increasingly demanding and at the same time independent and fickle:

"Well, yesterday I joined Esprit, for example. I like this brand and buy stuff from them quite frequently. I did it just because I wanted to state my preferences, and show my loyalty to these brands. However, it was the first reaction, and now I would like to see how it would benefit me in the future. I don't think following these companies on Facebook can make a big difference for me though."

"I find many products and services are superfluous in my life and ignore them but one, Gout Support, automatically made me 'Like' it. This is insidious. I have no interest in Gout support, despite my advanced years."

It comes with no surprise that often customers' relationships with brands in social media are influenced by the quality of their current brand experiences and the degree of your brand's relevance to them. In this respect, fickle relationships may be dictated by a lack of reasons for engagement with a brand, particularly if there is a relatively low degree of self-relevance.

Obliged Relational Bonds

Relational bonds between customers and brands could also be derived from statutory obligations, not because they are planned or wanted. The issue to explore here is why the customers' experiences with service providers are different from their experiences with product brands. Some customers feel that they are forced to keep in touch with banks or telecommunication services simply because they do not have a choice. One customer gave a very straightforward answer to why he would not follow Telecom NZ:

"No, they send me a bill every month."

It can be assumed that statutory obligations have a particular effect on the customer's attitude toward brands in a social media. Even though customers might have long-term relationships with a bank, your brand communications catalyst is likely to remain offline:

"I think it's very difficult for a bank to build a community around banking. It's kind of a necessary evil in a lot of ways."

Even though such relationships are mostly dictated by the necessity to stay informed on the news directly related to the customers' well being, it seems logical to suggest that these relationships are connected to functional consumption. Despite the lack of emotional or self-brand ties, the obliged relationships can still bring about a consumption value associated with service functionality by providing customers with convenient and accessible experiences.

Preexisting Relational Bonds

In many cases customers start engaging with brands in social media because of their preexisting, offline experiences. These relational bonds, identified as "Preexisting," may result in brand advocacy and loyalty. Preexisting relational bonds prevail over other forms of customer-brand relationships in social media. Customers are willing to continue communicating with brands that they have already established relationships with. Preexisting relationships tend to enhance service experiences in social media:

> "I've been a customer of Vodafone since my arrival in New Zealand. Obviously I'm with them for a long time, 7 years now. They provided me with my first Internet, my first cell phone and once they went to Facebook, I started following them because yep, I'm with Vodafone. Social media for them was a doddle. That also means they can do really cool stuff like giveaways and get a lot more reach because of the enormous loyalty they had before they went to social media."

The *5-Sources Model* also shows that advocacy and loyalty toward brands in social media are rooted in preexisting relational bonds. Giving the example of how Telecom NZ dealt with the public reaction to Stephen Fry's complaints regarding the quality of Telecom broadband on Twitter, a customer points out that:

> "Some people did back us up on that and say look, Telecom does do this well, which was nice. I think one of the key things for me was that the vast majority of the people that were abusing us were people that I'd never heard of, they weren't the people that we've actually interacted with and that I consider part of our little online community. So because we have built up relationships with people previously, they weren't the ones that were abusing us. If it was our own community turning on us then I would have found that a lot harder to take."

Preexisting relational bonds can be forged through the customers' involvement in online brand affiliations and in some cases produce emotional brand experiences. The example of Vodafone New Zealand illustrates that social media may enhance preexisting relationships through visualization and reinforcement of the customer's previous brand experiences.

Emerged Relational Bonds

Social media lets customers form new brand relations, often in response to their friends' recommendations or a direct invitation from a brand to join its brand community. Relational bonds that arise in social media without the support of previous offline experiences have been identified as "Emerged Relational Bonds."

The feedback from customers indicates that customers usually do not bond with businesses they do not have a history of relationships with. However, customers indicated a different type of relationship that often occurs in response to social media WOM. Relationships that have emerged for the first time in social media are often characterized by a low degree of self-relevance. In this light, the mode of brand engagement is not long lasting and is insignificant compared to preexisting relational bonds. As this customer argued:

> "One of my workmates, who also has another business outside of the consulting business he's got asked me if I could like her page and if I could tell my friends to like her page. I did like her page even though I have nothing to do with her business. I never looked at the page, but what I do on Facebook... Facebook gives you an option—you can hide posts, if you don't want to look at it every day."

However, if a new brand is congruent with the customers' interests, the newly emerging relationships may be developed further and lead to liking, interactivity, and cocreation...

> "I was looking through Indian clothes design pages, it interests me, because I love their clothing and their culture and one lady friend—requested me there, Mishka. And she was just beginning

her business. So I said... Let's see how I may help you. My friends they are quite active, they follow my wall for some reason. I would make a genuine comment on clothing she was designing, I supported her on the first three months and she has become a really good friend."

If a new brand is relevant to customers to a certain extent, the bonds that have emerged through the engagement with brands can be transformed into stronger relationships.

Casual Relational Bonds

Consumption practices in social media depend to a certain degree on the nature of a service. In this respect, customers' relationships with brands are shaped by the frequency of service usage, regardless of whether it is offline or online. Relations based on accidental or irregular experiences have been identified as "Casual Relational Bonds." From the customers' perspective, the intensity of brand-related communications in social media is largely dictated by the nature of the service, which is often oriented toward the customers' utilitarian needs:

"I have an insurance broker, I've tried to look him up, and he's not on any of the social media sites, so it's a good old-fashioned e-mail for him. Would I engage with him more if he were on Twitter? Probably not, you know it's the sort of thing you sign up once for and forget about it for a year or two, or until your circumstances change."

Even though the nature of some services implies a casual relationship, social media may shift the focus from the functional aspect of consumption and direct it toward the satisfaction of the customers' utilitarian, social and emotional needs, thus creating stronger relational bonds.

Closing Thoughts on the Relational Brand

The *5-Sources Model* argues that social media allow for interactivity and cocreation with brands, regardless of the physical and geographical location. Social media enables the customer's brand knowledge to be enhanced and they provide the opportunities to transform brand experiences into a relationship through personalized communications and cocreation.

The *5-Sources Model* revealed that personalized communications with a brand and engagement in brand-related activities constitute important forms of the relational aspect of consumption in social media.

The *5-Sources Model* also uncovered the different types of relational bonds that customers develop with brands depending on 1) the sense of personal relevance; 2) the nature of the service; 3) the need and frequency of communications, and 4) situational dependency.

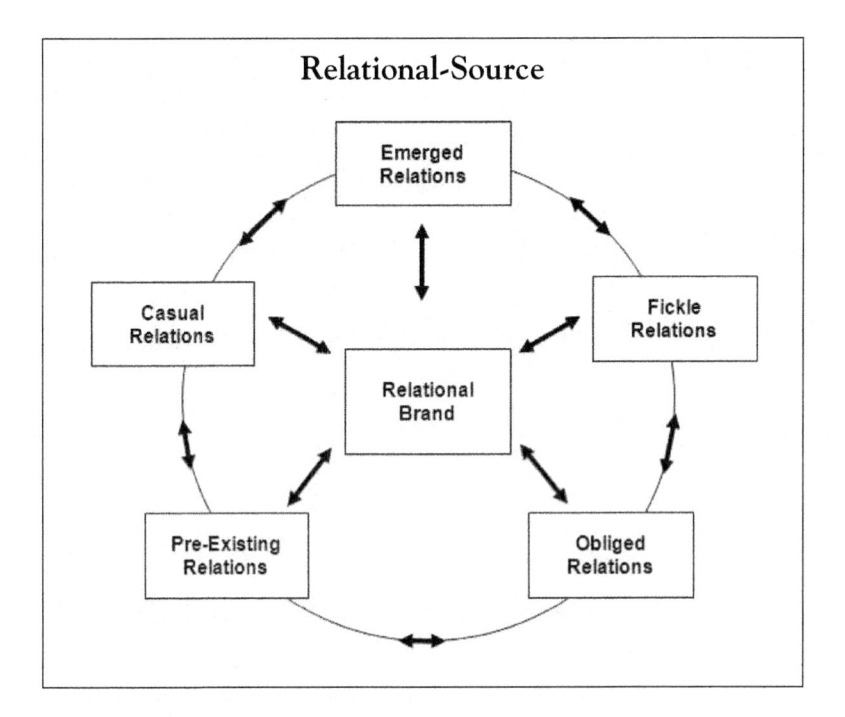

Relational-Source

- Emerged Relations
- Casual Relations
- Fickle Relations
- Relational Brand
- Pre-Existing Relations
- Obliged Relations

Personalized communication and cocreation creates engagement

The *5-Sources Model* shows that customers value social media communication with brands because it makes them part of the decision making process. Customers value the personal responses from your brand in the form of follow-up comments, likes, retweets or simply the acknowledgment of being a regular. Such engagement reinforces and acknowledges the importance of the customer as an individual to your brand.

The *5-Sources Model* argues that customers are ready to invest time and their own ideas by participating in your brands' opinion polls and discussions, for example, on new service initiatives. Social media make them feel like they have the authority to influence the businesses' practices. Customers also believe that, due to the properties of social media, their opinions are heard not only by your brands but the public as well. Customers help to cocreate the market offerings, taking the brand off in their own desired direction.

It can be said that interactivity and cocreation in social media contexts signify practices in which customers participate as brand coproducers, reviewers, or marketers. For some customers the outcome of the relationship with your brand is the possibility to choose service channels they can interact with at their own convenience. For others it is about building and linking your brand community.

Social media have shifted the focus from abstract forms of brand communications to close and personal ones. From the customers' perceptive, it means knowing the person behind your brand, which gives customers a sense of brand tangibility. Whatever the focus of the customers' interactivity with a brand in social media, it has a consequence that creates value. The benefits of interactivity and engagement with a brand are fostering individualized engagement and experience outcomes.

Although prior research has developed well-known typologies of customer-brand relationships, they can only be partially applied to a social media context[1]. Moreover, the forms of relationships produced by current studies are more or less extensions or modifications of existing typologies. There is also a gap in the understanding of customer-brand relationships in the community-oriented environment of social media. The *5-Sources Model* has identified that customers may be very fickle on social media channels. The consumption behavior of fickle customers is difficult to predict and manage because of the situational dependency of consumption practices. For example, customers may respond to sale promotions or available giveaways as well as to friends' recommendations.

---

[1] *See* for example, the important work of Fournier, S., Breazeale, M., and Fetscherin, M. (eds.) *Consumer-Brand Relationships: Theory and Practice*, Routledge, 430 pages, New York, USA.

The form of relationships in both cases is temporary and bonded to the present situation. For example, as soon as the promotion ends, customers stop interacting with your brand. Situations such as traveling or studying overseas also tend to determine fickle relationships.

The *5-Sources Model* shows that these circumstances may motivate customers to follow newspapers or airlines pages on Facebook and Twitter to gain insights about a new country. The issue to explore here is how these bonds can be transformed into longer-term reciprocal relationships. When the customer is fickle and unpredictable, predicting their behavior is not as important as to being able to react immediately to their new aspirations through the maintenance of a continuous relationship. Feedback from customers has identified that they may be involved with a brand in social media because of statutory obligations, not because the relationship is voluntary, planned, or wanted. Such relationships have been indentified in terms of financial and telecommunication services.

For example, a few customers say that they keep in touch with banks because they are kind of necessary evils in life. Even though it is not a common theme, it seems to be a relevant criterion for understanding how customers form relationships with banks and insurance, telecommunication, and power companies, as these services are considered to be absolute necessities and are considered responsible for people's well-being. Unfortunately, it was difficult to assess this book result due to the lack of knowledge relative to the relationships identified as obligatory.

The *5-Sources Model* argues that the customers' connection with a brand is often based on preexisting brand experiences, which is the most common case in social media. For example, it is common for many customers to continue their relationships with your brands with which they have long-term relationships. From the customers' perspective, social media give them another channel for communications with brands.

In general, the customers appreciate the social move from brands and some express regret at not being able to interact with favorite companies that do not have a social media presence. Customers with preexisting relationships demonstrate self-brand emotional connections and loyalty toward brands with which they have had previous offline experiences.

The preexisting relationship bonds that are illustrated in the *5-Sources Model* can to some extent be likened to the relationship called a marriage of convenience. It is a long-term relationship created by rules rather than choice. The *5-Sources Model* also pointed toward a brand loyalty resulting from preexisting relationships. There were several cases from long-time customers who advocated for BNZ bank and Telecom NZ on Facebook and Twitter in difficult situations. Social media as a network-oriented environment are assigned the task of connecting, which means developing new affiliations and relationships.

In this regard, the *5-Sources Model* identified a new type of relationship bond called emerged, which characterizes the customers' brand connections that occurred for the first time in social media. It should be noted that there is a strong temptation to define this type of relationship as fickle or casual, but the emerged relations are not necessarily unstable or time-bonded, they are just new. For example, it is found that customers might encounter brands by following a friend's recommendation.

Customers are also exposed to social media advertising or promotional campaigns. In many cases such brand engagement bear little or no relationship to individual customers unless a brand's characteristics are recognized by them as being relevant or familiar. There is an assumption that brand familiarity, defined as the reflection of previous brand experiences, impacts on consumption practices, including brand choice, evaluation, advertising, and WOM messages processing.

Finally, the *5-Sources Model* identified casual relational bonds formed by accidental or irregular brand experiences. Coming back to Fournier's (1998) typology, it seems that the description of the casual friends/buddies relationships is applicable to the social media context as well[2]. The casual friends/buddies form of customer-brand relationships is characterized by infrequent or sporadic engagement with few expectations for reciprocity or rewards, and the friendship is low in effect and intimacy.

The customers argues that they are likely to develop casual relationships with, for instance, insurance and home design companies as there is no need for regular contact. Interestingly, while customers' engagement with some brands has casual arrangements due to the nature of

---

[2] *See* Fournier, S. "Consumers and their Brands: Developing Relationship Theory in Consumer Research." *Journal of Consumer Research* 24, (March 1998): 343–73.

the business and the customers' lifestyles, it does not affect their attitude toward your brand. For instance, the customers note that they would not visit, for example, a Facebook home design brand community on a regular base, but would recommend this brand and continue using it if the occasion arose.

Therefore, in the context of social media, casual experiences can transfer into brand relationships because of brand visibility, accessibility, and positive WOM. However, this will be dependent on the congruence between your brands reputation and the customer's everyday life experiences.

CHAPTER 8

Implementing Social Media Branding

Create Functionality Through Product I Love, Service I Use

"If it's a brand I personally use, or have an interest in I'll follow them, so I follow Telecom on both Twitter and Facebook, and LinkedIn. Tip Top, coz I like their products."

Even a brief nonscientific observation of the customers' brand-related activities in social media could give an idea of how customers define their relationships with products and brands. Pinterest is a good example, where there are plenty of users' boards named "Product I Love" and there is little regard for services in this sense. In the conversation about brands in social media, customers recognize their functional characteristics in the first instance.

For example, the ability to quickly solve problems and find information has been identified as the most important factor. It is explained by the nature of the service, which is associated with a high-risk purchase situation, intangibility, and nonstandardized qualities. Long before there was social media, researchers were pointing to the need to tangibilize the offer by providing visible or exploratory cues that prospective service customers can use to evaluate the ultimate benefits and quality.

It should be acknowledged here that from the list of potential activities above, businesses tend to employ mostly the specials and giveaways approach, still considering social media as an additional channel for sales and advertising.

> **Functional-Source**
>
> - Material Rewards: Brand as a "priority club" enables customers to get an exclusive access to the material and tangible rewards.
> - Problem Solving: Brand as an "emergency room" focuses on a stress free, time and moneysaving solutions and enables customers to address problems as soon as they emerge.
> - Information Search: Brand as an "information center" enables customers to find required information about the brand, available alternatives and/or expert advice.
> - Knowledge: Brand as a "search engine" and a "data center" enables customers to manage knowledge about the brand in a convenient way.
> - Feedback: Brand as a "conference room" enables customers to express their opinions directly to brand.

In sum, brand functionality carries a value proposition by focusing on customer benefits in such aspects as a) time-saving and cost-effective problem solving; b) brand mobility and flexibility in providing customers with required information, customers' tips and quick-fixes; c) convenience and accessibility of consumption; d) attentiveness and responsiveness to customers' inquires, and e) rewards for customer engagement.

Create Emotion By Tapping Into My Feelings

"On Twitter it's so easy, I feel like I can talk to somebody and don't feel shy and not engaged."

The *5-Sources Model* shows that in some cases, brand engagement might be limited to the customers' utilitarian needs. But this does not mean that the same scenario applies to all consumption practices in social media. In this regard, marketing practitioners need to recognize the importance of the emotional aspect in brand consumption.

The model illustrates that customers look for enjoyable brand experiences, which are expected to be entertaining and include elements of humor, fantasy, or curiosity. By engaging with a brand in social media, customers may also overcome some personal problems, such as homesickness. Others use a brand as a form of aspirations, which is particularly true for the leisure, fashion, and travel industries. Helped to escape and manufacture rich memory.

Even though some of the customers' stories about their emotional experiences relate to product brands, they are provided here to show how entertaining and enjoyable experiences can be incorporated into social media strategies to give customers more than just practical reasons for interacting with brands.

Emotional-Source

- Curiosity: Brand as an object of curiosity. By holding a curiosity value brand makes customers want to "uncover" the brand.
- Enjoyment: Brand as a source of enjoyable and exciting experiences that makes customers feel happy and satisfied.
- Fantasy: Brand as a form of customer escapism, desired reality and aspirations offering exciting and unusual experiences.
- Entertainment: Brand as a source of entertainment. By giving customers amusements and interest brand makes them to enjoy their experiences.
- Privilege/Recognition: Brand as the source of reassurance that customers are noticeable and appreciated by a brand.
- Problem Alleviation: Brand as a source of help given customers to deal with personal difficult situations.

The *5-Sources Model* points to the fact that the value of consumption can also be attributed to emotional experiences, which are constructed through the activities customers, have undertaken to fulfill their emotional needs. They will also become more active in engagement and the experience of the brand, heightening the emotional response.

Create The Personal and Social

"If your brand fits with how you perceive yourself or how you want to be perceived, then you press "like.""

Traditionally, the notion of interconnections between the symbolic meanings of consumption and the customers' self-image is associated with product brands. However, should services, which are not material objects, be considered? Can customers still express themselves and show their attachment and relationship to others while experiencing a lack of physical brand presence? Customers suggest that using social media as the public domain may help to overcome some difficulties with regard to the intangible nature of services and also find new or reconsider existing solutions for the development of customer self-brand connections.

Self-Sourcing

- Life Arrangements: Brand as a source of support for customers to simplify or facilitate their day-to-day activities.
- Self-Relevance: Brand as a link to the customers' sense of self. Customers get involved with brand that fits well with their personal/professional interests and life style.
- Self-Branding: Brand as a platform for the customer self-branding, building and raising their social profiles.
- Self-Actualization: Brand as a source of support for customers to achieve what they want through their relationships with brand.
- Expression: Brand as a vehicle for self-expression which allows the customer to publically present their thoughts and ideas and let others know who and what they are.

If a brand wants to create meaningful experiences for customers or to attract their attention, it should understand that a customer' personal goals, values, and interests have to resonate with your brand meanings. The *5-Sources Model* shows that customers are willing to publicly continue their relationships with brands as long as they are congruent with their sense of self. Moreover, self-relevance may motivate customers to act as pivotals.

Create Relationship

"It can be a community hub . . . You are talking about florists, an under -12 rugby team, and your plan to have sausage a sizzle this weekend . . . ."

Obviously, since brands decided to go social they have become a part of the social media community. The question to ask here is whether they are able to bring customers a sense of community, as this is not just about lumping people together; it is about focusing on community interests, engagement, and link building. The *5-Sources Model* proposes that social media approaches need to be derived from an understanding of the role of the community, where consumption experiences are formed, shared, and communicated.

It seems logical to suggest that customers foster your brand relationship because it allows them to engage with society, sometimes at an intimate and personal level. At the same time, members participate because the communities are fun and enjoyable.

Social-sourcing

- Experience Exchange: Brand as a service for the exchange of experiences, ideas, and know-how between customers.
- Sociality: Brand as a meeting platform that gives customers a place to talk.
- Link Building: Brand as a source of the customer networking for personal or professional interests.
- Community Attachment: Brand as a community hub where customers experiences are formed, shared, and communicated.

Some customers are looking for a community of their favorite businesses in social media, such as car and hairdressing services, and they expect brands to be there. In this respect, social media silence from the service supplier carries a negative message for customers. Further, marketing practitioners need to understand that the boundaries between online and offline are blurring and any events that are happening today will be discussed tomorrow on Facebook, Twitter, Google +, and so on. In branding services, the main focus should be on creating a buzz around community-oriented activities, as Air New Zealand did by promoting the premier of The Hobbit movie.

Being Interactive and Personal

"I'm not now going to tell 40 of my friends to buy this product unless I believe in it. So what you've got to do is you've got to build the relationship up with me."

The *5-Sources Model* shows that all aspects of brand consumption are interrelated, but more importantly, they revolve around cocreation and interactivity between customers and brands.

Relational-Source

- Emerged: The form of relationships occurred for the first time in social media and based on online experiences only.
- Casual: The form of relationships resulting from accidental or irregular experiences regardless of online or offline context.
- Preexisting: The form of relationships resulting from customers' prior brand knowledge and experiences.
- Obliged: The form of relationships resulting from statutory obligations, not because it is wanted or desirable.
- Fickle: The form of relationships that is temporary and often bonded by the present situation.

In contrast to product brands, service experiences imply a greater customer involvement in brand production and consumption as they are created in dynamic brand relationships. This emphasizes the role of customer interactivity and bi-directional online communications in the building of brand reputation: customers taking control and it is changing brand image development. In this regard, the ultimate goal of social media strategies for brands is to improve customers' experiences and nurture relationships with them.

It is also important to keep in mind that social media produce not only new forms of consumption, but also new forms of relationships between brands and customers, which can be fickle, preexisting, emerged, casual, or obliged. Even though there are no ready-made ideas of how to transform obliged relationships into a voluntary union or how to predict the behavior of fickle customers, marketers in branding services should focus on personalized conversations with customers. The *5-Sources Model* shows that customers easily recognize hard selling marketing approaches in social media and resist engaging with forceful and self-focused brands.

Overall, the customers argue that the value of customer-brand relationships in social media should be delivered through useful, relatable, personal, human, assessable, and interactive consumption: the market is an engaged conversation between brands and their stakeholders.

Closing Thoughts

As we come to the end of this book the focus now shifts primarily to you, your brand, and your customers. The time to start developing and implementing the *5-Sources Model*. This will be a journey of discovery but I caution you to keep it simple. I ask that you most of all, listen to the customer and community and put them in control.

Five Sources of Value

So, remember the functional, the emotional, the self, the social, and the relational. All come together to make the *5-Sources Model*:

- **Functional:** It puts the customer back in control and enabled how the community can be enveloped into this process of value creation.
- **Emotional:** Your brand strategy will start to leverage the community in a new way to express collective feelings and emotional value. The brands emotive impact will have wide consequences

- **Self:** Your social media brand will start to develop its image that is more in line with community members.
- **Personal:** The brand that is starting to evolve will help to foster closer social linkages within the collective building more valued and meaningful reasons why your brand is truly loved.
- **Relational:** Finally, the brand will be the relationship as it evolves with the social media community. It is no longer a stand-alone observer. Now, the key participant that binds the community of relationships and defines relationship equity.

Build Engagement Through Community, Content, and Exchange

Start thinking about how your brand will start building that conversation with customers and the community. Focusing on the simplicity of the community, content, and exchange. It is the primary definition of social media community and the space in which your social media brand will breathe and evolve.

Build Engagement Through the Brand as Application (APP)

I also want you to think about the brand as an APP or the application. Traditional branding has its place, but technology now plays such a key role in engagement with customers and communities. The Smartphone is ubiquitous and this is not just a trend. The APP as the brand is only that start of that new approach. Now is the time to start adapting your brand to fit that model so that your brand will be as ubiquitous as your customers in social media.

Build Engagement Through Pivotals that Create Momentum

Think also about whom are your pivotals. The key customers that are going to drive and provide momentum for the flow of communications surrounding your social media brand.

Determine about the pivotals:

- How are they defined?
- What motivates them?

- How do you identify and target them in the customer/community mix?
- Embark on a journey of really getting to know them. Develop strategies that will reward them for their role in your social media brand.

Build Engagement Through the Length and Breadth of Conversations

We also talked about momentum as the length and breadth of conversations that surround your brand that your customers and stakeholders are engaging in. Together they make it viral. Length is time and breadth is the number of community members, pivotals, different horizontal communities and vertical channels of engagement (e.g., mobile, web, radio, tv, and so on) your conversations transcend.

Build Engagement Through Experimentation

Finally, mistakes. You are going to make them because you will be experimenting. In the short term when customers and community are in increasing control, things may seem chaotic and random. They probably are! The best things you can do are listening and learning. Then develop and apply. I would also encourage you to post a question to the blog for this book through drrobertdavis.com. What social media branding says, and it is predominant in the *5-Sources Model,* is that this is a continual process. There is no beginning and no end.

So! Just start.

CHAPTER 9

Brand Building in Action

The *think* part of the book is where you start to do some further structured thinking about your brand using some of the case examples that have been developed. The eight cases I have included focus on the following areas:

- Case One: Looks at *Social Media Branding for Small Business* by focusing on the small business with "Yarns with Erica and Jess." It is what I call an everyday case showing how simple it is to develop and implement a social media branding strategy that encompasses the *5-Sources Model*.
- Case Two: Examines how *Social Media Spreads using the Westjet' Christmas Cheer Around the World* campaign. This is an example where offline and online community are used in synergy. This campaign went viral and we could like to explore how this happened. Viral activity is a great way to quickly get some initial attention to your social media brand.
- Case Three: *Fun with Bitstrips* discusses the issue about whether we can introduce other types of content into the brand communication and social media community. I ask you to consider the fun element of comics can be used as part of that content. You may consider other fun content to increase the emotional component of the brand.
- Case Four: There is a shift *Toward Informal Communication and Social Media*. This has implications for internal communication. Some companies are replacing the Inbox with secure social media communication applications. I ask you to think about moving away from e-mail. Maybe it is time to think about how the *5-Sources Model* can be applied internally.

- Case Five: *Banking and Social Media Relationship*s are a good example of the reinforcement of faceless contact. I consider how companies can avoid this paradigm. The *5-Sources Model* is all about developing a personal engagement with your brand. Don't become so seduced by the power of the technology that you forget the primary aim of the social media brand.
- Case Six: *Offline Engagement and Online Community* is a vital strategy to ensure that both market spaces work together. Often companies have an either/or approach. The emphasis on one at the expense of the other. This case explores how the on and offline spaces can be coupled to optimize your brands interactive experience.
- Case Seven: Often with technology we can forget about the *Human Factor in Social Media*. I argue that it is time to think about the person in social media strategy.
- Case Eight: This case is about changing the brand from traditional market orientations toward a brand that is more community and social media centric.

Case 1

Yarns with Erica and Jess

Social Media Branding for Small Business: Yarns with Erica and Jess

Today was a really great day for me. Just a normal winter's day in Auckland, New Zealand. My son and I decided to go and have a walk to the village. Have a coffee and do some shopping. Raining and cold! We stopped in at a local church that had a craft day on in Mt. Eden. I was looking around and then it hit me and I immediately thought about the book I have been working on focusing on social media branding for small business.

The stall was pretty simple. Two women aged in their early 20's smiling and doing knitting. Wow, they also had eft-pos. But the sign

BRAND BUILDING IN ACTION 93

was brilliant on many levels. Apart from being very witty, that is, the yarns part playing off knitting and chatting, I loved the link to Facebook. Wow, They get it. Social media branding is really simple. In a witty way linking the offline brand and conversation with the social media community based conversation.

And, yes, what is the outcome for their brand. We spent $35. We have told over 500 people. . .

Cool. So, go and have a yarn. Yarns with Erica an d Jess.

Questions

1. What are some of the key success factors in their social media strategy?
2. In this and other cases, how do you think you can translate engagement into transactions?

Case 2

Westjet Xmas Cheer

Social Media Spreads Westjet' Christmas Cheer Around the World by Inna Piven

Social Media Spreads WestJet' Christmas Cheer Around the World

Being heavily involved in social media marketing, sometimes I find it difficult to separate personal taste and professional judgment on what brands do regarding social media. In the case of WestJet's Christmas Real-Time Giving campaign, which went viral, I was in perfect harmony with myself. If you somehow missed the story—watch it on YouTube.

During last week, my news feeds on Facebook and Twitter were full of posts and reposts in different languages about WestJet's Christmas initiative, simply because it put smile on people's faces and raised their spirits. The number of views on the video speaks for itself—25,584,159 views on YouTube in 6 days! Frankly speaking, the whole idea of giving passengers of two Calgary-bound flights specific Christmas gifts that they wanted is smart, fresh, and creative.

A typical comment on the video would be:

"I saw the video posted on Facebook by my husband and a friend. Wow! I cried! That was the best Christmas "flash mob" "surprise" or "That, is honestly the nicest thing I have ever seen a business do." I find now a days there is no more customer service and this really showed me that someone really cares."

Following many businesses on social media, I was looking for big and exciting Christmas ideas this year, taking into account that the power of social media has finally been recognized. However, this year, again it is all about discounts, coupons, and sales in general. It seems like we ignore the true meaning of being social on social media—it is not about sales; it is about communication.

The good news is that WestJet's Christmas story can be implemented on a much smaller scale.

- A great customer involvement—making them participate, putting people together.
- Make consumers happy—by doing that, there is a chance to create emotional bonds.
- Help consumers solve some problems—look at the family in the video who was presented a big screen TV.
- Acknowledge consumers—a small token of appreciation can go a long way.
- Don't think sales, think relationships (that's why the WestJet campaign didn't look like a traditional PR idea).

If all five points are involved and creatively designed, your consumers and social media will do the work for you, spreading your story to the global community.

Questions

1. Why do you think this campaign went viral?
2. How did WestJet couple online and offline channels together to create engagement?

Case 3

Fun with Bitstrips

Comical Fun: Bitstrips

Don't you just love <u>Bitstrips?</u> It is not often used by brands in social media. We think there is an opportunity here. Why?

Cool story, bro.

This is because Bitstrips enables four key components of the *5-Sources Model.*

Source 1: Emotional Social Media Brand: it helps the brand express emotion in a fun and indirect way. It depersonalizes it in many ways. As the character evolves so does the emotions.

Source 2: Self-Orientated Social Media Brand: it allows the brand to evolve the self. Often brands are seen as flat impersonal worlds. Why not characterize them in this real virtual space. The self can be as same or as different to your customers.

Source 3: Personal Experience Social Media Brand: as customers start to engage with the characters and cartoons; dialogue is created. The brand can learn about the experiences of the consumer. They can respond to them and be part of that experience. This is how relationships evolve.

Source 4: Relational Social Media Brand: why can't unreal cartoons be a real basis for a relationship? Take the brand out of the functional.

Try it. Why not use Bitstrips in your social media? Create a character and start to play.

Questions

1. If you were to create a comic character for your brand, what would its characteristics be? Why are these important?
2. Go to Bitstrips and have a go at creating your character. Ask your customers for feedback.

Case 4

Communication and Social Media

Replace the Inbox with Social Media by Inna Piven

Sarwant Singh, BBC business author, in his article on megatrends that will change everyone's lives predicts a shift toward more informal collaboration in our workplace on a base of social media. According to him, social media tools will replace the inbox by 2020.

Well, it seems like old news to me—social media is not a new kid in town any longer. Just look at your message box on Facebook or Twitter. A lot of my communications go online, either with my business partners, colleagues, or my students. Moreover, while doing my research on social media branding, I used Facebook and Twitter to reach companies I wanted to interview. I didn't spend time googling their contact details and writing long formal business letters.

Can we use this current trend toward informal communication in business and if so, how? Let your consumers talk to you on social media, not just in a form of comments and likes, but via messages. Check messages on your business page regularly, the same way you check your inbox. It's important to reply the same day (I know from my personal experience that it's quite easy to ignore messages on social media).

Your consumers are very attentive audience, so a delay in replying, not to mention avoidance will be noticed. Besides, if they sent you a message on social media there is definitely a reason for that (they may have not been able to reach you by phone or e-mail). That's the beauty of social media—it's time-saving solution not only for your consumers, but for you as well. And more importantly it reduces the distance between your businesses and your consumers.

Isn't that what you try to achieve?

Questions

1. What does your staff think about using social media for informal communication? What are the arguments for and against this idea?
2. What type of applications does your staff mostly use when they engage in informal communications?

Case 5

Banking and Social Media

Relationships and Faceless Contact by Inna Piven

Guess Who. Source 5—Relations

Do you accept friend requests from people with fanciful avatars? I have a collection of unsorted friend requests from cats, knights, celebrities, and all kind of strange creatures. The point that is always stressed in this regard—the use of an avatar frees some people from shyness; it helps them to express themselves more openly. How about businesses?

It comes as no surprise that businesses have everything to do with their brands (logos, slogans, information, offerings, announcements), but not with real people who represent the brand in social media. The desire to articulate the brand is quite understandable, but who do I talk to?

As a consumer I don't want to interact with a faceless organization. The situation businesses are confronted with now is how to build relationships with the audience—that's why a human touch to social media branding is really necessary. After all, the audience wants to know who is behind the avatar with the brand logo on it.

One solution is to let customers know the brand's community manager(s). For instance, how ASB bank does it on Twitter (screenshot). BNZ used the same approach, but recently they excluded this information from their social media profiles and not for the good.

Questions

1. If you started to engage more in social media, what areas pose most of the risk in becoming too faceless in your communication with customers?
2. What strategies would you employ to reduce these risks?

Case 6

Offline Engagement and Online Community

Social Media Presence Offline by Inna Piven

Recently I came across heavy criticism against putting icons of Facebook, Twitter, Pinterest, or other networks on a company's front door or windows.

A blogger I follow questioned if such approach makes any sense to consumers. "What's the point of inviting me to find you on Facebook, while I'm in your office right now?"—The blogger asked.

Well, let's not overcomplicate a simple matter. Businesses with an established online presence should advertise its social media profiles—it's important to show consumers where they can reach you, besides your office or website. What are the benefits? Firstly, you show a social side of your business (open, friendly, and communicative). Secondly, by coupling your offline activities with online ones, you gradually build a community around your business. Thirdly, by blurring the line between consumers' online and offline interaction you make their experiences more engaging.

So, taking into account the complexity of consumers' brand experiences, announce your social media profiles both online and offline. For instance, a sign saying "Find US ON..." can be put on your blog or website, printed ads (brochures and flyers), TV ads, business cards, in-house posters, and, of course, on windows and front doors.

However, before putting social media icons on your front door make sure that your profile is very much alive.

Questions

1. How do you currently use the offline market space in your marketing communications and other business activities?
2. Of these approaches, choose three that could be used with social media to complement the offline strategies.

Case 7

The Human Factor

Social Media—Putting the hr Back by Inna Piven

It comes with no surprise that many of us consider LinkedIn a main source for professional networking and job seeking. Not only do we invest a considerable amount of time in self-branding on LinkedIn, building attractive profiles, searching for the right people and companies to connect with and writing an employer-friendly CV, recruitment agencies also believe that LinkedIn simplifies their tasks in searching for the right candidates.

Recently I have been involved in a project which researched the question if job seekers actively use social media to stay connected to recruitment agencies? If so, what do they look for and what implications might it have? Results from a focus group with job seekers were clear and expected: social media is a reliable instrument for recruitment purposes. However, the idea of "staying in touch" with recruitment agencies seems more appropriate for Facebook rather than LinkedIn. For example, the majority of the project participants pointed out that:

- They expect recruitment agencies to be on Facebook;
- They would prefer to receive regular updates via Facebook (job vacancies, and so on.)
- As one participant said ". . . there is no need to redirect me on (recruitment agency) website, I'm already here (on Facebook), on your business page."
- They don't mind if the recruitment agency checks their personal Facebook profile;
- They expect regular communications with recruitment agents on Facebook as well as with other job seekers;
- They would like to see success stories and share their own.
- Obviously, social media poses a challenge on the existing order of things in the recruitment industry and HR sector. It's about time Facebook brought into recruitment strategies.

Questions

1. Think about your recruitment and talent strategies? Describe the current approach in detail.
2. How could this approach be deployed online using LinkedIn or Facebook?

Case 8

Not Much Spark in Spark.co.nz

This case is about changing the brand from traditional market orientations toward a brand that is more community and social media centric.

I was very excited about the change of brand from Telecom NZ to SPARK. It was about time that they moved into the future and changed that core brand promise. Cool. The problem is with the change is that it appears the organization has not changed. This was particularly true of our experience of the front line sales staff in a SPARK retail store over the weekend.

So here is the proposition for SPARK at the moment. When you make such a large change in brand promise, it is important to retain your customers and in particular, your loyal customers. It is obvious 101 Marketing and branding. It is even more important when you are changing your brand from its traditional market orientations toward a brand that is more community and social media centric. Customers get nervous about those changes. Loyal ones are most concerned because often they will feel that they are going to be forgotten. Often, competitors will also be circling them with great offers because they know they are vulnerable.

Case in point is a customer called Janine. This is your dream customer. Been loyal to Telecom NZ for 30 years. Spends well over $100/month. Using land-line, broadband, and mobile. Pays on time, everytime those bills. Engages in regular WOM. Is loyal despite the fact they have never reviewed her account or services. I call this a ticking time bomb of disloyal.

Here is the problem or opportunity: Janine wants to upgrade her phone, broadband, and so on. Hence, we go into SPARK to get a good deal, knowing that she may have to pay more but is under the firm belief that they will reward her for her loyalty to gain her loyalty for the next 30 years.

Well unfortunately SPARK does not see it that way. In the 10 minutes interaction with the sales staff Janine experienced the following:

1. Arrogance and indifference and being told, "OK, you can go to Vodafone if you want to".
2. An approach that nearly brought my partner to tears. Always bad to make the customer cry.
3. Inflexibility in sales offering. Take it or leave it Model T Ford approach.
4. A confused sales approach.

5. Absolutely no respect or recognition for the Superloyal Customer.
6. Complete lack of understanding of the SPARK brand and the messages behind the current campaigns talking about "Starting" and saying "Thanks".
7. Finally, if that sales person called me *mate* again (in a rude way) I was going to scream!

Janine left pretty gutted. So, Janine went to Vodafone and here is what happened:

1. We got a new Samsung 5 plus new SIM card for FREE.
2. Doubled the mobile data plus free texts and calls.
3. Double the broadband data plus new modem etc.
4. Got rid of the land-line.
5. A great sales approach and service. Sam was a really nice guy. Professional and will go far in marketing.
6. All content moved from old phone to new phone.
7. Discount on accessories.
8. Screen protector installed.
9. Paying about the same but about $15/month more. A bottle of wine.
10. Vodafone has the pleasure of deleting SPARK.
11. But most of all—A VERY HAPPY NEW CUSTOMER—who will probably be loyal for the next 30 years. Who will pay their bills on time. Who will engage in position WOM. Nothing more to say really except it is Branding 101.

If you make a promise through the brand. Deliver on it. Every-time. Every-way. Everywhere. Most importantly, your people are a massive part of the brand promise but vitally, its delivery. It is their approach that defines the optimal customer experience and value.

It is the Sam's of this world who create the platform of WOM. LOL because I know Janine has already told her story to about 40 people so far. In the next 30 years this story will be retold to tell people how important customers are and to Janine, how important she is. This is her mantra. For Janine it was clear and simple. SPARK did not care. Vodafone cared and most importantly wanted her valued business. Go Nino!

Questions

1. Thinking about changes you are going to make to your brand in the future to ensure it becomes more community oriented. How will you ensure that traditional front line face to face delivery will be maintained and enhanced?
2. What incentives will you provide your loyal customers to continue to be loyal as your brand shifts to being social media centric?
3. For your loyal customers, how will you convert them from simply being loyal to becoming active pivotals in the collective communications model. *See* Chapter 2 for more in pivotals.

Suggested Readings

Alba, J., Lynch, J., Weitz, B., Janiszewski, C., Lutz, R., Sawyer, A., and Wood, S. "Interactive Home Shopping: Consumer, Retailer and Manufacturer Incentives to Participate in Electronic Marketplaces." *Journal of Marketing* 61, no. 3 (1997): 38–53.

Arnould, E. J., and Price, L. L. "River Magic: Extraordinary Experience and the Extended Service Encounter." *Journal of Consumer Research* 20, (1993): 24–45. http://www.jstor.org

Bagozzi, R. P., and Dholakia, U. M. "Intentional Social Action in Virtual Communities." *Journal of Interactive Marketing* 16, no. 2 (2002): 2–21.

Balasubramanian, S., Peterson, R. A., and Javenpaa. S. L. "Exploring the Implications of M-Commerce for Markets and Marketing." *Journal of Academy of Marketing Science* 30, no. 4 (2002): 348–61.

Barnes, S. J. "Wireless Digital Advertising: Nature and Implications." *International Journal of Advertising* 21, no. 3 (2002): 399–420.

Barnes, S. J. "The Mobile Commerce Value Chain. Analysis and Future Developments." *International Journal of Information Management* 22, no. 2 (2002a): 91–108.

Barwise, P., and Farley, J. U. "The State of Interactive Marketing in Seven Countries: Interactive Marketing Comes of Age." *Journal of Interactive Marketing* 19, no. 3 (2005): 67.

Barwise, P., and Strong, C. "Permission-Based Advertising." *Journal of Interactive Marketing* 16, no. 1 (2002): 14–24.

Beer, D., and Burrows, R. "Consumption, Prosumption and Participatory Web Cultures." *Journal of Consumer Culture* 10, no. 3 (2010): 3–12.

Belk, R. W. "Situational Variables and Consumer Behaviour." *Journal of Consumer Research* 2, (1975): 157–64. http://dbe.cc/pub/Consumer%20Behaviour/Belk_1976.pdf

Belk, R. W., and Tumbat, G. "The Cult of Macintosh. Consumption." *Markets and Culture* 8, no. 3 (2005): 205–17.

Belk, R. W., Wellendorf, M., and Sherry, J. J. "The Sacred and the Profane in Consumer Behaviour: Theodicy on the Odyssey." *Journal of Consumer Research* 16, (1989): 1–38.

Berry, L. L. "Cultivating Brand Equity." *Journal of the Academy of Marketing Services* 28, no. 1 (2000): 128–37. http://jam.sagepub.com

Berry, L. L., and Seltman, K. D. "Building a Strong Services Brand: Lessons from Mayo Clinic." *Business Horizons* 50, (2007): 199–209.

Berry, L. L., Seiders, K., and Grewal, D. "Understanding Service Convenience." *Journal of Marketing* 66, no. 3 (2002): 1–17. http://www.jstor.org

Bezjian-Avery, A., and Calder B. "New Media Interactive Advertising Vs. Traditional Advertising." *Journal of Advertising Research* 38, no. 4 (1998): 23–33.

Biyalogorsky, E., Gerstner, E. and Libai, B. "Customer Referral Management: Optimal Reward Programs." *Marketing Science* 20, no. 1 (2001): 82–95.

Breazeale, M. "Word of Mouth: An Assessment of Electronic Word-of-Mouth Research." *International Journal of Market Research* 51, no. 3 (2009): 297–318.

Brodie, R. J., Glynn, M. S., and Little, V. "The Brand and the Service-Dominant Logic: Missing Fundamental Premise or the Need for Stronger Theory?" *Marketing Theory* 6, no. 3 (2006): 363–79.

Brodie, R. J., Hollebeek, L. D., Juric, B., and Ilic, A. "Customer Engagement: Conceptual Domain, Fundamental Propositions, and Implications for Research." *Journal of Service Research* 14, no. 3 (2011a): 252–71.

Brodie, R. J., Ilic, A., Juric, B., and Hollebeek, L. "Consumer Engagement in a Virtual Brand Community: An Exploratory Analysis." *Journal of Business Research* 66, no. 1 (2011b): 105–14.

Brown, J., Broderick, A. J., and Lee, N. "Word of Mouth Communication within Online Communities: Conceptualizing the Online Network." *Journal of Interactive Marketing* 21, no. 3 (2007): 2–20.

Caru, A., and Cova, B. "Small Versus Big Stories in Framing Consumption Experiences." *Qualitative Market Research: An International Journal* 11, no.2 (2008): 166–76.

Catterall, M., and Maclaran, P. "Researching Consumers in Virtual Worlds: A Cyberspace Odyssey." *Journal of Consumer Behaviour* 1, no. 3 (2002): 228–37.

Chakrabarti, R., and Berthon, P. "Gift Giving and Social Emotions: Experience as Content." *Journal of Public Affairs* 12, no. 2 (2012): 154–61.

Chan, K. K., and Misra, S. "Characteristics of the Opinion Leader: A New Dimension" *Journal of Advertising* 19, no. 3 (1990): 53–60.

Chau, P. Y. K., Cole, M., Massey, A. P., Montoya-Weiss, M., and O'Keefe, R. M. "Cultural Differences in the Online Behavior of Consumers, Association for Computing Machinery." *Communications of the ACM* 45, no. 10 (2002): 138–43.

Cheung, C. M. K., Lee, M. K. O., and Rabjohn, N. "The Impact of Electronic Word-of-Mouth: The Adoption of Online Opinions in Online Customer Communities." *Internet Research* 18, no. 3 (2008): 229–247.

Clarke, I., III. "Emerging Value Propositions for M-Commerce." *Journal of Business Strategies* 18, no. 2 (2001): 133–48.

Coulter, R. A., Price, L. L., and Feick, L. "Rethinking the Origins of Involvement and Brand Commitment: Insights from Postsocialist Central Europe." *Journal of Consumer Research* 30, no. 2 (2003): 151–169.

Cova, B., and Pace, S. "Brand Community of Convenience Products: New Forms of Customer Empowerment—The Case My Nutella the Community." *European Journal of Marketing* 40, no. 9/10 (2006): 1087–1105.

Cova, B. "Community and Consumption towards a Definition of the Linking Value of Product or Services." *European Journal of Marketing* 31, (3/4), (1997): 297–316.

Coviello, N. E., Milley, R., and Marcolin, B. "Understanding IT-Enabled Interactivity in Contemporary Marketing." *Journal of Interactive Marketing* 15, no. 4 (2001): 18–33.

Coviello, N. E., Roderick. J. B., Danaher, P. J., and Johnston, W. J. "How Firms Relate to their Markets: An Empirical Examination of Contemporary Marketing Practices." *Journal of Marketing* 66, no. 3 (2002): 33–46.

Da Silva, R. V., and Alwi, S. F. "Online Brand Attributes and Online Corporate Brand Images." *European Journal of Marketing* 42, no. 9/10 (2008): 1039–58.

Danaher, P. J., Wilson, I. W., and Davis, R. A. "A Comparison of Online and Offline Consumer Brand Loyalty." *Marketing Science* 22, no. 4 (2003): 461–76.

Danaher, P. J., Hardie, B. G. S., and Putsis, W. P., Jr. "Marketing-Mix Variables and the Diffusion of Successive Generations of a Technological Innovation." *Journal of Marketing Research* 38, (November 2001): 501–14.

Davis, R. A. "Conceptualizing Fun in Mobile Commerce Environments." *International Journal of Mobile Communications* 8, no. 1 (2010): 21–40.

Davis, R. A. and Chaudhri, A. "Conceptualizing Play in Mobile Commerce Environments." *International Journal of Mobile Marketing* 7, no. 2 (2012): 65.

Davis, R. A. and Sajtos, L. "Measuring Consumer Interactivity in Response to Campaigns Coupling Mobile and Television Media." *Journal of Advertising Research* 48, no. 3 (2008): 375–91.

Davis, R. A., and Yung, D. "Understanding the Interactivity between Mobile Commerce and Television Environments." *Communications of the ACM* 48, no. 7 (July 2005): 103–5.

Davis, R. A., Piven, I., and Breazeale, M.. "A Conceptual Model of Consumers Service Brand Consumption in Social Media Community." *Journal of Retailing and Consumer Services* 21, no. 4 (2014): 468–81.

Davis, R. A., and Lang. B. "Does Perceived Control Increase Game Usage and Purchase Behaviour?" *International Journal of Consumer Research* 1, no. 1 (2012): 47–69.

Davis, R. A., and Lang, B. "Modelling Game Usage and Purchase Behaviour: The Consumption Value of Self Efficacy." *Journal of Retailing and Consumer Services* 19, (2011): 67–77.

Davis, R. A., and Lang, B. "Modelling Game Usage, Purchase Behaviour and Ease of Use." *Entertainment Computing* 3, (2011): 27–36.

Davis, R. A., and Lang, B. "Does Self-Congruity Increase Game Usage and Purchase?" *Young Consumers* 14, no. 1 (2013): 52–66.

Davis, R. A., Buchanan–Oliver, M. and Brodie R. J. "Retail Service Branding in Electronic–Commerce Environments." *Journal of Service Research* 3, no. 2 (2000): 178–86.

Davis, R. A., Buchanan–Oliver, M., and Brodie, R. J. "Relationship Marketing in Electronic Commerce Environments." *Journal of Information Technology* 14, no. 4 (1999): 319–31.

Davis, R. A., Lang, B., and Gautam, I. (2013). "Modelling Utilitarian-Hedonic Dual Mediation (UHDM) in the Purchase and Use of Games." *Internet Research* 23, no. 2 (2013): 229–56.

Davis, R. A., Lang, B., and San Diego, J. (2014). "Does Gender Matter in the Relationship between Hedonic Shopping Motivation and Purchase Intentions?" *Journal of Consumer Behaviour* 13, (2014): 18–30.

Davis, R. A., Laszlo Sajtos and Ahsan Chaudhri. "Do Consumers Trust Mobile Service Advertising?" *Contemporary Management Research* 7, no. 4 (2012): 245–70.

De Chernatony, L., and Dall'Olmo Riley, F. D. "Experts' Views about Defining Brands and the Principles of Services Branding." *Journal of Business Research* 46, no. 2 (1999):181–92. http://www.sciencedirect.com

De Chernatony, L., and Segal-Horn, S. (2001). "Building on Services' Characteristics to Develop Successful Brand." *Journal of Marketing Management* 17, (2001): 645–69. http://www.emeraldinsight.com

De Kerckhove, A. "Building Brand Dialogue with Mobile Marketing." *International Journal of Advertising & Marketing To Children* 3, no. 4 (2002): 37–43.

Dholakia, R. R., and Nikhilesh D. "Mobility and Markets: Emerging Outlines of M-Commerce." *Journal of Business Research* 57, (2004): 1391–96.

Drosses, D., Geroge M. G., George L., Flora K., and Maira G. S. "Determinants of Effective SMS Advertising: An Experimental Study." *Journal of Interactive Advertising* 7, no. 2 (2007): 16–27.

Duncan, T. and Sandra, E. M. "A Communication-Based Marketing Model for Managing Relationships." *Journal of Marketing* 62, no.2 (1998): 1–14.

Escalas, J. E., and Bettman, J. R. "Self-Construal, Reference Groups, and Brand Meaning." *Journal of Consumer Research* 32, no. 3 (2005): 378–89. http://www.jstor.org

Etgar, M. A Descriptive Model of the Consumer Co-Production Process." *Journal of Academy of Marketing Science* 26, (2008): 97–108.

Feenberg, A., and Bakardjieva, M. "Virtual Community: No Killer Implication." *New Media and Society* 6, no. 1(2004): 37–43.

Feng Li. "Who is talking? An Ontology-Based Opinion Leader Identification Framework for Word-of-Mouth Marketing in Online Social Blogs." *Decision Support Systems* 51, no. 1 (2011): 190–97.

Ferris, M. "Insight on Mobile Advertising, Promotion, and Research. *Journal of Advertising Research* 47, no. 1(March 2007): 28–37.
Firat, A. F. "The Consumer in Postmodernity." *Advances in Consumer Research* 18, (1991): 70–6. http://web.ebscohost.com.libproxy.unitec.ac.nz
Fischer, E., and Reuber, A. R. "Social Interaction via New Social Media: (How) can Interactions on Twitter Affect Thinking and Behavior?" *Journal of Business Venturing* 26, (2011): 1–18.
Fournier, S. "Consumers and Their Brands: Developing Relationship Theory in Consumer Research." *Journal of Consumer Research* 24, (1998): 343–73. http://www.jstor.org
Fournier, S., and Lee, L. "Getting Brand Communities Right." *Harvard Business Review* 87, no. 4 (April 2009): 105–111.
Gardner, M. P. "Mood States and Consumer Behavior: A Critical Review." *Journal of Consumer Research* 12, no. 3 (1985): 281–301.
Gerstheimer, O., and Lupp, C. "Needs Versus Technology—the Challenge to Design Third-Generation Mobile Applications." *Journal of Business Research* 57, (2004): 1409–15.
Grönroos, C. "Creating a Relationship Dialogue: Communication, Interaction, Value." *Marketing Review* 1, no. 1 (2000): 5–14.
Grönroos, C. "The Perceived Service Quality Concept—A Mistake?" *Managing Service Quality* 11, no. 3 (2001): 150–2. http:// www.emeraldinsight.com
Grönroos, C. "The Relationship Marketing Process: Communication, Interaction, Dialogue, Value." *Journal of Business & Industrial Marketing* 19, no. 2 (2004): 99–113.
Grönroos, C. "Adopting a Service Logic for Marketing." *Marketing Theory* 6, no. 3 (2006): 317–33.
Grove, J. S., and Fisk, P. R. "The Service Experience as Theater." *Advances in Consumer Research* 19, (1992): 455–61.
Gummesson, E. "All Research is Interpretive." *Journal of Business and Industrial Marketing* 18, no. 6/7 (2003): 482–92.
Haeckel, S. H. "About the Nature and Future of Interactive Marketing." *Journal of Interactive Marketing* 12, no. 1 (1998): 63–71.
Haig, M. *Mobile Marketing: The Message Revolution.* London: Kogan Page, 2002.
Heinonen, K. "Consumer Activity in Social Media: Managerial Approaches to Consumers' Social Media Behavior." *Journal of Consumer Behaviour* 10, (2011): 356–64.
Heinrichs, J. H., Lim, J.-S., and Lim, K.-S. "Influence of Social Networking Site and User Access Method on Social Media Evaluation." *Journal of Consumer Behaviour 10*, no. 6 (2011): 347–355.
Helkkula, A. "Characterizing the Concept of Service Experience." *Journal of Service Management* 22, no. 3 (2011): 367–89.

Hennig-Thurau, T., Malthouse, E. C., Friege, C., Gensler, S., Lobschat, L., Rangaswamy, A., and Skiera, B. "The Impact of New Media on Customer Relationships." *Journal of Service Research* 13, no. 3 (2010): 311–30.

Hirschman, E. C., and Holbrook, M. B. "Hedonic Consumption: Emerging Concepts, Methods and Propositions." *Journal of Marketing* 46, (1982): 92–101.

Hirschman, E. C. "Role-Based Models of Advertising Creation and Production." *Journal of Advertising* 18, no. 4 (1989): 42–53.

Hoffman, D. L. and Novak, T. P. "Marketing in Hypermedia Computer-Mediated Environments: Conceptual Foundations." *Journal of Marketing* 60, no. 3 (1996): 50–68.

Hoffman, D. L., and Novak, T. P. *Why Do People Use Social Media? Empirical Findings and a New Theoretical Framework for Social Media Goal Pursuit.* Social Science Research Network. Accessed January 17, 2012. http://papers.ssrn.com/sol3/papers.cfm?abstract_id=1989586

Holbrook, M. B., and Hirschman, E. C. "The Experiential Aspects of Consumption: Consumer Fantasies, Feelings, and Fun." *Journal of Consumer Research* 9, no. 2 (1982): 132–40.

Holbrook, M. B., Robert. W. C., and Greenleaf, E. "Play as a Consumption Experience: The Roles of Emotions, Performance, and Personality in the Enjoyment of Games." *Journal of Consumer Research* 11, no. 2 (1984): 728–40.

Holt, D. B. "How Consumers Consume: A Typology of Consumption Practices." *Journal of Consumer Research* 22, (1995): 1–17.

Homer, P. M., and Yoon, S-G. "Message Framing and the Interrelationships among Ad-Based Feelings, Affect, and Cognition." *Journal of Advertising* 21, no. 1 (1992): 19–34.

Houston, M. B., and Walker, B. A. "Self-Relevance and Purchase Goals: Mapping a Consumer Decision." *Journal of the Academy of Marketing Science* 24, no. 3 (1996): 232–45.

Hoyer, W. D., Chandy, R., Dorotic, M., Krafft, M., and Singh, S. S. "Consumer Cocreation in New Product Development." *Journal of Service Research* 13, no. 3 (2010): 283–96.

Hudson, L. A., and Ozanne, J. L. "Alternative Ways of Seeking Knowledge in Consumer Research." *The Journal of Consumer Research* 14, no. 4 (1988): 508–21.http:// www.jstor.org

Jones, M. A., Reynolds, K. E., Weun, S., and Beatty, S. E. "The Product-Specific Nature of Impulse Buying Tendency." *Journal of Business Research* 56, (2003): 505–11.

Kleijnen, M., De Ruyter, K., and Wetzels, M. "Consumer Adoption of Wireless Services: Discovering the Rules, While Playing the Game." *Journal of Interactive Marketing* 18, no. 2 (2002): 51–61.

Kohler, T., Füller, J., Stieger, D., and Matzler, K. "Avatar-Based Innovation: Consequences of the Virtual Co-creation Experience." *Computers in Human Behavior* 27, (2011): 160–68.

Kozinets, R. V. "Utopian Enterprise: Articulating the Meanings of Star Trek's Culture of Consumption." *Journal of Consumer Research* 28, (2001): 67–88.

Kozinets, R. V. *Netnography: Doing Ethnographic Research Online*. Los Angeles: Sage, 2010.

Kozinets, R. V. "Networked Narratives: Understanding Word-of-Mouth Marketing in Online Communities." *Journal of Marketing* 74, no. 2 (2010): 71–89.

Kozinets, R. V., Hemetsberger, A., and Schau, H. J. The Wisdom of Consumer Crowds: Collective Innovation in the Age of Networked Marketing." *Journal of Macromarketing* 28, no. 4 (2008): 339–54.

Kozinets, R. V. "E-Tribalized Marketing? The Strategic Implications of Virtual Communities of Consumption." *European Management Journal* 17, no. 3 (1999): 252–64. http://www.sciencedirect.com

Hairong, L., Daugherty, T., and Biocca, F. "Characteristics of Virtual Experience in Electronic Commerce: A Protocol Analysis." *Journal of Interactive Marketing* 15, no. 3 (2001): 13–30.

Li, M., Dong, Z.Y., and Chen, X. "Factors Influencing Consumption Experience of Mobile Commerce: A Study From Experiential View." *Internet Research* 22, no. 2 (2012):120–41.

Liu, Y., and Shrum, L. J. "What is Interactivity and is it always Such a Good Thing? Implications of Definition, Person, and Situation for the Influence of Interactivity on Advertising Effectiveness." *Journal of Advertising* 31, no. 4 (2002): 53–64.

Lovelock, C., and Gummesson, E. "Whither Services Marketing?: In Search of a New Paradigm and Fresh Perspectives." *Journal of Service Research* 7, no. 1 (2004): 20–41.

Lu, H., and Su, P. Y. "Factors Affecting Purchase Intention on Mobile Shopping Web Sites." *Internet Research* 19, no. 4 (2009): 442–58.

Madupu, V., and Cooley, D. O. "Antecedents and Consequences of Online Brand Community Participation: A Conceptual Framework." *Journal of Internet Commerce* 9, (2010):127–47.

Magura, B. "What Hooks M-Commerce Customers?" *MIT Sloan Management Review* 44, no. 3 (2003): 9.

Mahajan, V., Muller, E., and Bass, F. M. "New Product Diffusion Models in Marketing: A Review and Directions for Research." *Journal of Marketing* 54, (1990): 1–26.

McAlexander, J. H., Schouten, J. W., and Koenig, H. F. "Building Brand Community." *Journal of Marketing* 66, no. 1 (2002): 38–54.

McCracken, G. "Culture and Consumption: A Theoretical Account of the Structure and Movement of the Cultural Meaning of Consumer Goods." *Journal of Consumer Research* 13, no. 1 (1986): 71–84.

McDonald, M. H. B., de Chernatony, L., and Harris, F. "Corporate Marketing and Brands: Moving Beyond the Fast-moving Consumer Goods Model." *European Journal of Marketing* 35, no. 3/4 (2001): 335–52. http://www.emerald-library.com

McMillan, S. J., and Hwang, J. S. "Measure of Perceived Interactivity: An Exploration of the Role of Direction of Communication, User Control, and Time in Shaping Perceptions of Interactivity." *Journal of Advertising* 31, no. 3 (2002): 29–42.

McMillan, S. J. "A Four-Part Model of Cyber Interactivity: Some Cyber-Places are More Interactive than Others." *New Media and Society* 4, no. 2 (2002): 271–91.

Meraz, S. "Is There an Elite Hold? Traditional Media to Social Media Agenda Setting Influence in Blog Networks." *Journal of Computer-Mediated Communication* 14, (2009): 682–707.

Merisavo, M., Kajalo, S., Karjaluoto, H., Virtanen, V., Salmenkivi, S., Raulas, M., and Leppäniemi, M. "An Empirical Study of the Drivers of Consumer Acceptance of Mobile Advertising." *Journal of Interactive Advertising*, (2007): 261–77.

Merz, M. A., He, Y., and Vargo, S. L. "The Evolving Brand Logic: A Service-Dominant Logic Perspective." *Academy of Marketing Science*, (2009): 328–44. doi:10.1007/s11747-009-0143-3

Mick, D. G., and Bhul, C. "A Meaning-Based Model of Advertising Experiences." *Journal of Consumer Research* 19, (1992): 317–38.

Mittal, B., and Lassar, W. M. "The Role of Personalization in Service Encounters." *Journal of Retailing* 72, no. 1 (1996): 95–110.

Morgan-Thomas, A., and Veloutsou, C. "Beyond Technology Acceptance: Brand Relationships and Online Brand Experience." *Journal of Business Research*. doi:10.1016/j.jbusres.2011.07.019

Muniz, A. M. Jnr., and O'Guinn, T. C. "Brand Community." *Journal of Consumer Research* 27, (2001): 412–32.

Nambisan, P., and Watt, J. H. "Managing Customer Experiences in Online Product Communities." *Journal of Business Research* 64, (2011): 889–95.

Nysveen, H., Pedersen, P. E., Thorbjørnsen, H., and Berthon, P. "Mobilizing the Brand: The Effects of Mobile Services on Brand Relationships and Main Channel Use." *Journal of Service Research* 7, no. 3 (2005): 257–76.

Nysveen, H., Pedersen, P. E., Thorbjørnsen, H. "Intentions to Use Mobile Services: Antecedents and Cross-Service Comparisons." *Journal of the Academy of Marketing Science* 33, no. 3 (2005): 1–17.

O'Cass, A., and Grace, D. "Exploring Consumer Experiences with a Brand." *Journal of Product and Brand Management* 13, no. 4 (2004): 257–68.

Okazaki, S. "Social Influence Model and Electronic Word of Mouth." *International Journal of Advertising* 28, no. 3 (2009): 439–72.

Okazaki, S. "The Tactical Use of Mobile Marketing: How Adolescents' Social Networking Can Best Shape Brand Extensions." *Journal of Advertising Research* 49, no. 1 (March 2009): 12–26.

Ostrom, A. L., Bitner, M. J., Brown, S. W., Burkhard, K. A., Goul, M., Smith-Daniels, V., Demirkan, H., and Rabinovich, E. "Moving Forward and Making the Difference: Research Priorities for the Science of Service." *Journal of Service Research* 13, no. 1 (2010): 4–36.

Ouwersloot, H., and Odekerken-Schroder, G. "Who's Who in Brand Communities—and Why?" *European Journal of Marketing* 42, no. 5/6 (2008): 571–85.

Paavilainen, J. *Mobile Business Strategies: Understanding the Technologies and Opportunities.* London: Wireless Press, 2001.

Padgett, D., and Allen, D. "Communicating Experiences: A Narrative Approach to Creating Brand Image." *Journal of Advertising* 26, no. 4 (1997): 49–62. http://www.emeraldinsight.com

Pantzar, M. "Tools or Toys—Inventing the Need for Domestic Appliances in Postwar and Postmodern Finland." *Journal of Advertising* 32, no. 1 (2003): 83–93.

Parasuraman, A., Zeithaml, V. A., and Berry, L. L. "A Conceptual Model of Service Quality and its Implications for Future Research." *Journal of Marketing* 49, (1985): 41–50. http://www.cob.unt.edu

Patterson, A. "Social-networkers of the World, Unite and Take Over: A Meta-introspective Perspective on the Facebook Brand." *Journal of Business Research* 65, no. 4 (2011): 527–34.

Pauleen, D., and Yoong, P. "Facilitating Virtual Team Relationships via Internet and Conventional Communication Channels." *Internet Research: Electronic Networking Applications and Policies* 11, no. 3 (2001): 190–202.

Payne, A., Storbacka, K., Frow, P., and Knox, S. "Co-creating Brands: Diagnosing and Designing the Relationship Experience." *Journal of Business Research* 62, (2009): 379–89.

Prahalad, C. K., and Ramaswamy, V. "Co-creation Experiences: The Next Practice in Value Creation." *Journal of Interactive Marketing* 18, no. 3 (2004): 5–14.

Rafaeli, S. "Interactivity from new media to communication." In *Advancing Communication Science: Merging Mass and Interpersonal Processes,* edited by Hawkins, R. P., Wiemann, J. M., and Pingree, S., 110–34. Beverly Hills, CA: Sage.

Ritson, M., and Elliot, R. "The Social Uses of Advertising: an Ethnographic Study of Adolescent Advertising Audiences." *Journal of Consumer Research* 26, no. 3 (1999): 260–78.

Ritson, M., and Elliot, R. "A Model of Advertising Literacy: the Praxiology and Co-Creation of Advertising Meaning," 24th EMAC Conference Proceedings, (May 1995), 1035–54.

Schmitt, P., Bernd, S., and Van den Bulte, C."Why Customer Referrals Can Drive Stunning Profits." *Harvard Business Review* 89, no. 6 (2011): 30.

Schouten, J. W. "Selves in Transition: Symbolic Consumption in Personal Rites of Passage and Identity Reconstruction." *Journal of Consumer Research* 17, no. 4 (1991): 412–25.

Schouton, J. W., and McAlexander, J. H. "Subcultures of Consumption: An Ethnography of the New Bikers." *Journal of Consumer Research* 22, (1995): 43–61.

Schumann, D. W., Artis, A., and Rivera, R. "The Future of Interactive Advertising Viewed Through an IMC Lens." *Journal of Interactive Advertising* 1, no. 2, (2001). http://jiad.org/vol1/no2/Schumann

Shankar, V., Venkatesh, A., Hofacker, C., and Naik, P. "Mobile Marketing in the Retailing Environment." *Current Insights and Future Research Avenues* 24, (2010): 111–20.

Shankar, V., and Balasubramanian, S. "Mobile Marketing: A Synthesis and Prognosis." *Journal of Interactive Marketing* 23, no. 2, (2009): 118–29.

Shao, G. "Understanding the Appeal of User-Generated Media: A Uses and Gratification Perspective." *Internet Research* 19, no. 10 (2009): 7–25.

Shih, T. F. "Conceptualizing Consumer Experiences in Cyberspace." *European Journal of Marketing* 32, no. 7/8 (1998): 655–63.

Simmons, G. "Marketing to Postmodern Consumers: Introducing the Internet Chameleon." *European Journal of Marketing* 3, no. 4 (2008): 299–310.

Solomon, M. R. "The Role of Products as Social Stimuli: A Symbolic Interactionism Perspective." *Journal of Consumer Research* 10, (1983): 319–29.

Stern, B.B. "A Revised Communication Model for Advertising. Multiple Dimensions of the Source, the Message, and the Recipient." *Journal of Advertising* 23, no. 2 (1994): 5–15.

Stern, B. B., Zinkhan, G. M., and Holbrook, M. B. "The Netvertising Image: Netvertising Image Communication Model (NICM) and Construct Definition." *Journal of Advertising* 31, no. 3 (2002): 15–27.

Steuer, J. "Defining Virtual Reality: Characteristics Determining Telepresence." *Journal of Communication* 42, no. 4 (1992): 73–94.

Sultan, F., and Rohm, A. J. "The Evolving Role of the Internet in Marketing Strategy: An Exploratory Study." *Journal of Interactive Marketing* 18, no. 2 (2004): 6–19.

Sundaram, D. S., and Webster, C. "The Role of Brand Familiarity on the Impact of Word-of-mouth Communication on Brand Evaluations." *Advances in Consumer Research* 26, (1999): 664–70.

Sundqvist, S., Frank, L., and Puumalainen, K. "The Effects of Country Characteristics, Cultural Similarity and Adoption Timing on the Diffusion of Wireless Communications." *Journal of Business Research* 58, no. 1 (2005): 107–10.

Taylor, C. R., Lee, D-H. "New Media: Mobile Advertising and Marketing." *Psychology & Marketing* 25, no. 8 (2008): 711–13.

Thompson, C., Locander, W. B., and Pollio, H. R. "Putting Consumer Experience Back into Consumer Research: The Philosophy and Method of Existential-Phenomenology." *Journal of Consumer Research* 16, (1989): 133–46.

Toffler, A. *The Third Wave*. New York, NY: Bantam Books, 1980.

Tonteri, K., Kosonen, M., Ellonen, H-K., and Tarkiainen, A. "Antecedents of an Experienced Sense of Virtual Community." *Computers in Human Behavior* 27, no. 6 (2011): 2215–23.

Toral, S. L., Martinez-Torres, M. R., Barrero, F., and Cortes, F. "An Empirical Study of the Driving Forces behind Online Communities." *Internet Research* 19, no. 4 (2009): 378–92.

Trappey, R. J. and Woodside, A. "Consumer Responses to Interactive Advertising Campaigns Coupling Short-Message-Service Direct Marketing and TV Commercials." *Journal of Advertising Research* 45, no. 4 382–401.

Tsanga, A. S. L., and Zhoub, N. "Newsgroup Participants as Opinion Leaders and Seekers in Online and Offline Communication Environments." *Journal of Business Research* 58, no. 9 (2005): 1186–93.

Tuominen, P. "Emerging Metaphors in Brand in Brand Management: Towards a Relational Approach." *Journal of Communication Management* 11, no. 2 (2007): 182–91.

Van Dijk, J., and De Vos, L. "Searching for the Holy Grail: Images of Interactive Television." *New Media and Society* 3, no. 4 (2001): 443–65.

Vargo, S. L., and Lusch, R. F. "Evolving to a New Dominant Logic for Marketing." *Journal of Marketing* 68, no. 1 (2004): 1–18.

Vargo, S. L., and Lusch, R. F. "The Four Service Marketing Myths: Remnants of a Goods-based, Manufacturing Model." *Journal of Service Research* 6, no. 4 (2004): 324–35.

Vargo, S. L., and Lusch, R. F. "Service-dominant Logic: Continuing the Evaluation." *Journal of the Academy of Marketing Science* 36, (2008): 1–10.

Veloutsou, C. "Brands as Relationship Facilitators in Consumer Markets." *Marketing Theory* 9, no. 1 (2009): 127–30.

Veloutsou, C., and Moutinho, L. "Brand Relationships through Brand Reputation and Brand Tribalism." *Journal of Business Research* 62, (2009): 314–22.

Watson, R. T., Leyland F. P., Berthon, P., and Zinkhan, G. M. "U-Commerce: Expanding the Universe of Marketing." *Journal of the Academy of Marketing Science* 30, no. 4 (2002): 333–47.

Westbrook, R. A., and Oliver, R. L. "The Dimensionality of Consumption Emotions: Patterns and Consumers Satisfactions." *Journal of Consumer Research* 18, no. 1 (1991): 84–91.

Wikström, S. R. "A Consumer Perspective on Experience Creation." *Journal of Consumer Behavior* 7, no. 1 (2008): 31–50.

Wolfgang, P., Key, P., and Dietmar, G. W. "Mobile Word-Of-Mouth—A Grounded Theory of Mobile Viral Marketing." *Journal of Information Technology* (Palgrave Macmillan) 24, no. 2 (2009): 172–85.

Woodside, A. G., and Delozier, M. W. "Effects of Word of Mouth Advertising on Consumer Risk Taking." *Journal of Advertising* 5, no. 4 (1976): 12–19.

Zeithaml, V. A., Parasuraman, A., and Berry, L. L. "Problems and Strategies in Service Marketing." *Journal of Marketing* 49, (1985): 33–46. http://www.jstor.org

Zeithaml, V. A., Parasuraman, A., and Malhotra, A. "Service Quality Delivery through Web sites: A Critical Review of Extant Knowledge." *Journal of the Academy of Marketing Science* 30, no. 4 (2002): 358–71.

Zhang, X., and Prybutok, V. R. "How the Mobile Communication Markets Differ in China, the U.S., and Europe, Association For Computing Machinery." *Communications of the ACM* 48, no. 3 (2005): 111–14.

Index

Accessibility, 32, 36–37
Apple, 2, 4

Brand. *See also* 5-Sources Model; Social media branding
  as application, 11–13, 88
  building in action, 91–104
  communities, 21–23
  self-branding, 7, 51–52, 54–56, 84

Casual relational bonds, 9, 75, 86
Colgate, 16
Collective relationships, 8–9
Community(ies)
  attachment, 8, 61–62, 66–67, 85
  brand, 21–23
  reboot, 1–2
Consumption, 17
CCE. *See* Content, community, and exchange (CCE)
Content, community, and exchange (CCE), 14, 15–19, 88
Convenience, 32, 36–37
Conversations, length and breadth of, 89
Curiosity, 5, 43–44, 47, 83

Disney, 11, 12

Emerged relational bonds, 9, 74–75, 86
Emotional social media brand, 3–5, 29–30, 39–47
  creating, 82–83
  curiosity, 5, 43–44, 47, 83
  enjoyment, 5, 39–41, 45–46, 83
  entertainment, 5, 40–41, 45–46, 83
  fantasy, 5, 43, 46, 83
  privilege, 5, 42–43, 47, 83
  problem alleviation, 5, 41–42, 46, 83
Enjoyment, 5, 39–41, 45–46, 83
Entertainment, 5, 40–41, 45–46, 83

Experience exchange, 8, 59–61, 65–66, 85
Experimentation, 89
Expression, 7, 84

Facebook, 6, 8, 9, 13, 14, 16, 25, 26, 35, 36, 37, 40, 42, 55, 56, 57, 61, 66, 67, 78, 79, 80, 85, 101
Fantasy, 5, 43, 83
Feedback, 3, 25–31, 36, 82
Fickle relational bonds, 9, 71–72, 86
5-Sources Model
  emotional social media brand, 3–5, 29–30, 39–47, 82–83
  functional social media brand, 2–3, 25–38, 81–82
  personal (social) media brand, 7–8, 59–67, 86–87
  relational social media brand, 8–9, 69–80, 85–86
  self-oriented social media brand, 5–7, 49–58, 84
Functional social media brand, 2–3, 25–38
  convenience and accessibility, 32, 36–37
  creating, 81–82
  feedback, 3, 25–31, 36, 82
  information search, 3, 25–31, 36, 82
  knowledge, 3, 33–34, 37, 82
  material rewards, 3, 82
  problem solving, 3, 25–31, 36, 82
  prompt action, 31–32, 36–37
  rewards, 34–35, 37–38
Functional vs. emotional aspects, of brand consumption, 19–21

Google, 2, 3
Google +, 85

Her, 8
Hershey's, 9
Honda, 18

IKEA, 15
Information search, 3, 25–31, 36, 82

Jobs, Steve, 4

Knowledge, 3, 33–34, 37, 82

Learning experiences, engagement through, 30–31
Life arrangements, 7, 53–54, 57–58, 84
Link building, 8, 62–63, 66–67, 85
LinkedIn, 8, 26, 100, 101

Material rewards, 3, 82
Mayo Clinic, 20–21
McDonald's, 16

NTT Docomo, 18

Obliged relational bonds, 9, 72, 86

Pepsi, 15
Personalized brand communication, 70–71
Personal life context, 27–28
Personal (social) media brand, 7–8, 59–67, 86–87
  community attachment, 8, 61–62, 66–67, 85
  creating, 86–87
  experience exchange, 8, 59–61, 65–66, 85
  link building, 8, 62–63, 66–67, 85
  social engagement, 8, 64, 85
Pinterest, 20, 44, 81, 99
Pivotals, 88–89
Preexisting relational bonds, 9, 73–74, 86
Privilege, 5, 42–43, 47, 83
Problem alleviation, 5, 41–42, 46, 83
Problem solving, 3, 25–31, 28–29, 36, 82
Prompt action, 31–32, 36–37

Relational social media brand, 21–23, 69–80, 85–86
  casual relational bonds, 9, 75, 86
  emerged relational bonds, 9, 74–75, 86
  fickle relational bonds, 9, 71–72, 86
  obliged relational bonds, 9, 72, 86
  personalized brand communication, 70–71, 76
  preexisting relational bonds, 9, 73–74, 86
Rewards, 34–35, 37–38

Self-actualization, 49–50, 54–56, 84
Self-branding, 7, 51–52, 54–56, 84
Self-expression, 7, 54–56
Self-oriented social media brand, 5–7, 49–58
  creating, 84
  expression, 7, 84
  life arrangements, 7, 53–54, 57–58, 84
  self-actualization, 7, 49–50, 54–56, 84
  self-branding, 7, 51–52, 54–56, 84
  self-relevance, 7, 50–51, 56–57, 84
Self-relevance, 7, 50–51, 56–57, 84
Siemens, 20
Social engagement, 64
Sociality, 8, 85
Social media branding. *See also* Brand; 5-Sources Model
  content, community, and exchange, 15–19
  functional vs. emotional aspects of, 19–21
  importance of, 11–24
  relationships and community, 21–23
SMC. *See* Social media community (SMC)
Social media community (SMC), 13–15

Target and Woolworths, 13
Time of customers, valuing, 26–27
Twitter, 25, 26, 31, 35, 36, 37, 55, 56, 57, 61, 66, 67, 73, 78, 79, 85, 94, 97, 99

Volkswagen, 18

Walmart, 2, 12

Xero Live, 26

OTHER TITLES IN OUR DIGITAL AND SOCIAL MEDIA MARKETING AND ADVERTISING COLLECTION

Vicky Crittenden, Babson College, Editor

- *Viral Marketing and Social Networks* by Maria Petrescu
- *Herding Cats: A Strategic Approach to Social Media Marketing* by Andrew Rohm and Michael Weiss
- *Effective Advertising Strategies for Your Business* by Cong Li
- *Social Roots: Why Social Innovations Are Creating the Influence Economy* by Cindy Gordon, John P. Girard, and Andrew Weir

FORTHCOMING IN THIS COLLECTION

- *A Beginner's Guide to Mobile Marketing* by Karen Mishra
- *Using and Managing Online Communities* by Edward Boon
- *Electronic Word of Mouth for Service Businesses* by Linda W. Lee
- *Fostering Brand Community Through Social Media* by Debra A. Laverie, Shannon B. Rinaldo, and William F. Humphrey, Jr.
- *Digital Marketing Management: A Handbook for the Current (or Future) CEO* by Debra Zahay

Announcing the Business Expert Press Digital Library

Concise e-books business students need for classroom and research

This book can also be purchased in an e-book collection by your library as

- a one-time purchase,
- that is owned forever,
- allows for simultaneous readers,
- has no restrictions on printing, and
- can be downloaded as PDFs from within the library community.

Our digital library collections are a great solution to beat the rising cost of textbooks. e-books can be loaded into their course management systems or onto student's e-book readers.
The **Business Expert Press** digital libraries are very affordable, with no obligation to buy in future years. For more information, please visit **www.businessexpertpress.com/librarians.** To set up a trial in the United States, please contact **Adam Chesler** at adam.chesler@businessexpertpress.com. For all other regions, contact **Nicole Lee** at nicole.lee@igroupnet.com.